1 MONTH OF
FREE
READING

at
www.ForgottenBooks.com

By purchasing this book you are eligible for one month membership to ForgottenBooks.com, giving you unlimited access to our entire collection of over 1,000,000 titles via our web site and mobile apps.

To claim your free month visit:
www.forgottenbooks.com/free921773

ISBN 978-0-260-00737-7
PIBN 10921773

═First Annual Meeting═

MONROE, LA.

MAY 10-14, 1911

Woman's

Missionary Society

Louisiana Conference

Methodist Episcopal Church, South.

PREFATORY

With the prospect of the unificaton of the Home Mission and the Foreign Missionary Societies, a joint session of these organizations was held in Monroe, May 10-14, 1911, bringing in closer bond of Christian fellowship the delegates of these bodies, the presidents employing alternate days for discussion of the work of their departments.

The presence of Miss Bennett the two first days and that of Miss Head through the closing sessions, gave energy and inspiration to the Conference, making this one of the most profitable ever held. In a short talk Wednesday morning, Miss Bennett's clear and forceful explanation of the decisions of the Woman's Council prepared the delegates for intelligent action, and to unanimously voice their wish for a united society. Wednesday night a welcome to Monroe from the church was extended by the pastor, Rev. R. H. Wynn, and by the Auxiliaries through Mrs. M. A. McHenry. The response for the delegates, by Mrs. S. A. Montgomery, in short, pithy sentences was enjoyed by all.

The annual addresses of the presidents, Mrs. Kennedy and Mrs. Carre, gave a brief synopsis of the work and the outlook in their departments. Miss Bennett brought a message filled with giving a "whole gospel to the whole world," telling incidents of its fruit-bearing in China and Korea as well as in our home land.

Thursday evening was given Miss Bennett and Rev. N. E. Joyner. The devotional service was led by Rev. S. S. Keener, D.D. Miss Bennett made a strong appeal for "service-winners," as well as "soul-winners and the study of God's Word," knowing, then doing God's will.

An object lesson was given by Rev. N. E. Joyner, through his stereopticon slides, of conditions about St. Mark's Hall, which Miss Ragland, deaconess in charge, explained. The beautiful music by the choir was a feature of the evening service.

A large congregation met Friday night to hear Rev. A. S. Lutz on the Ministry of the Deaconess, text Romans xvi, 1-2, as he gave historical facts of the revival of the primitive order, the office being a practical necessity of modern life, closing with an eloquent appeal for the service.

Miss Head arrived in the afternoon and was introduced to the Conference, acknowledging it in a few words of greeting.

No meeting was held Saturday night.

Sunday morning Miss Head talked to the young people of the Sunday School, her theme, "Missions—the Duty and Necessity of the Work."

Rev. Paul Brown filled the pulpit for the Conference sermon, his text being the incident when the Master, with basin and towel, washed the disciples' feet, "giving Christianity its badge," love the motive power and through infinite love the salvation of man. In the afternoon Miss Head and Miss Ragland talked to the children, teaching and interesting as well.

At night Miss Head filled the evening with a talk on the Jubilee Meetings now being held throughout our land, in celebration of the fiftieth anniversary of the organization of the first Woman's Missionary Society. Miss Head called this the greatest day of the greatest age of the world, because we are so near the world's redemption, adding the shortest road to Korea, China or a city's slums, is by way of prayer! In conclusion of this service, Mrs. D. C. Worrell read resolutions of thanks to all who had in any way contributed to the success of this Conference. (See resolutions.)

FIRST ANNUAL MEETING

of the

WOMAN'S MISSIONARY SOCIETY

OFFICIAL MINUTES.

MONROE, LA., May 9, 1911, 9:30 A. M.

The nineteenth annual session of the Woman's Home Mission Society was called to order by the President, Mrs. E. R. Kennedy. Hymn No. 408, "Lead On, O King Eternal," was sung and Mrs. T. S. Randle led in a fervent prayer. A psalm was read responsively. Mrs. Kennedy made an inspirational talk and the many dear voices responding to the call told of God's blessing and loving care during the year just past.

The Secretary called the roll and read the rules of order. The President announced her committees. The following resolution prevailed:

"Resolved, That every member of this body shall have a voice and a vote on all matters, home and foreign, coming before the conference during the present session, and that the first business be the discussion of the union of the two conference societies.

"MRS. S. A. MONTGOMERY.

"MRS. CROW GIRARD."

Mrs. Montgomery announced that Miss Bennett was present, and the President asked her to come forward. The conference was glad to welcome the President of the Woman's Missionary Council and enjoyed her brief greeting. Miss Bennett was made temporary chairman and the conference went into a meeting of the committee of the whole. Mrs. Montgomery read the law as given by the council to govern a united conference society. Mrs. Carre, Mrs. Montgomery, Mrs. Kennedy, Mrs. A. P. Holt, Mrs. Snelling and many others spoke to the question. It was unanimously decided to unite the two conference societies.

The following resolution was then presented:

·"Resolved, That we recommend that where practicable the
auxiliaries of the Home and Foreign departments unite into one
society and adopt the constitution and by-laws suggested by the
Woman's Missionary Council.

"MRS S. A. MONTGOMERY."

Mrs. R. C. Holt read the constitution as recommended for
the auxiliaries. Miss Bennett explained the duties of the Social
Service Vice-President and made many interesting and lucid
explanations of the new law. The decision was unanimous in
favor of this resolution.

Mrs. Kennedy resumed the chair and the committee of the
whole made its report.

It was decided to begin the daily sessions at 9·o'clock and
to close at 12 o'clock, the afternoon session to begin at 2 o'clock
and a business session to be held after the memorial service.

Rev. N. E. Joyner came forward to conduct the noontime
Bible study. He spoke of the fact that every Englishman's mind
was turning at this season to old England on account of the
coronation, and drew a beautiful analogy between this and the
coronation of him who is the Lord and Master of us all. His
words of encouragement and advice were helpful, indeed. After
a prayer, Rev. S. S. Keener pronounced the benediction.

AFTERNOON SESSION.

The service was in memory of our beloved and sainted co-
worker, Ruth Reams Sandlin. Hymn No. 463, "Jesus, Lover of
My Soul," was sung. Mrs. Kennedy, Mrs. Girard, Miss Mary
Werlein, Mrs. T. S. Randle, Mrs. R. C. Holt, Mrs. Holmes,
Mrs. Will Lewis and others spoke in loving remembrance of
this dear one. Mrs. Fuller read an article from the Minden
paper and spoke of the loss of her friend.

The following resolution was read by Mrs. Kennedy:

"In the death of Mrs. John N. Sandlin, our Third Vice-
President, our conference society has lost one of its most valued
and earnest workers. Lovely in person, bright and gifted and
young, her going away brings to each one of us a sense of personal loss; and our hearts ache with the thought that her voice
is missing from our counsels and her sweet personality is known

no more in our midst. But, while our hearts are filled with sadness, let us lift up our eyes to the hills from whence cometh our help! May our faith enable us to look beyond our loneliness and sorrow to her blessed home with Jesus! May we realize that our God 'doeth all things well' and that our cherished friend has only gone on before, in the brightness of her young life, forever free from disappointment and care and the burdens of this life.

"Whereas, this sorrow has come to us, be it resolved that our conference society express deepest sympathy to her bereaved and heart-broken family, to the church of which she was a valued member and to the friends who loved and depended upon her. Let us resolve to be more faithful in the work she loved so well— that of enlisting the children for Christ and bringing their young lives into his blessed service; that a copy of these resolutions be placed in our annual report and a copy sent to the family.

"Signed:
"MRS. E. R. KENNEDY.
"MRS. R. C. HOLT.
"MRS. R. H. WYNN.
"MRS. CROW GIRARD.
"MRS. H. R. SINGLETON."

The singing of "Nearer My God to Thee" closed this solemn service.

The President called for the Treasurer's report. It was read and accepted.

The Auditor's report was read and adopted.

Rev. R. W. Vaughan was presented to the conference and spoke of the Orphanage. The conference Corresponding Secretary made her report and it was adopted. A motion was made and carried that the committees made at the morning session be annulled and that joint committees be formed by the executive committees from both the Home and Foreign Departments. Mrs. Kennedy then gave some interesting news from the recent council meeting in St. Louis.

The Credentials Committee made its report.

Announcements were made, the Doxology was sung and the benediction was pronounced by Rev. T. S. Randle.

THURSDAY MORNING.

The first session of the Foreign Mission work under the new adjustment was opened with singing "The Son of God Goes Forth to War." Scripture lesson from I Thes. and voluntary prayers, filled with hunger for the Christ-life. Calling the roll and reading the rules for delegates was next in order. The minutes of meetings ad. interim were accepted. The Corresponding Secretary moved that statistical reports of auxiliaries be omitted, giving each delegate the privilege of adding comments to that of the District Secretary, amended by Mrs. Girard, moving the matter be left to the discretion of the Presidents; carried.

The report of the Corresponding Secretary, filled with information and evidencing the faithful performance of duty, was accepted, save the promise of $1000.00 as a part of the $75,000.00 expected of the women of Southern Methodism toward the Jubilee Fund. This was left to a committee.

The Treasurer's report was read and adopted, showing an increase of receipts throughout the State; the Auditor's certificate of approval was adopted.

Miss Bennett told of the wonderful power of the Gospel in China and Korea, and urged pledges rather than specials as evidence of the missionary spirit; also explained the Retirement Fund as an obligation to the aged and infirm deaconesses and missionaries. Committees were announced as follows:

Credentials—Mrs. R. H. Wynn, Mrs. J. M. Munholland, Mrs. J. W. Walter.

Courtesies—Mrs. R. H. Wynn, Mrs. W. M. Terry, Mrs. S. M. Handy, Mrs. J. T. Bryant, Mrs. J. W. Johnston.

Publication—Mrs. A. C. McKinney, Mrs. H. C. Blanks, Mrs. Lawson McDonald, Miss Fannie Reams, Miss Mattie Hooper.

Finance—Mrs. R. C. Holt, Mrs. J. J. Holmes, Mrs. H. D. Causey, Miss Addie Ferguson.

Resolutions—Mrs. D. C. Worrell, Mrs. H. S. Edwards, Mrs. L. W. Fuller, Mrs. Oscar Chapman, Mrs. A. L. Crowson.

Young People's Work—Miss M. Ragland, Miss Edna Doll, Miss Sadie Pipes, Miss Belle Tankersley, Miss Hattie Renfroe, Miss Florence Philips, Miss Mattie Holt, Miss Mattie Lawrence, Mrs. S. C. Lloyd, Mrs. J. C. Allen, Mrs. A. I. Townsley, Miss Nellie Bynum, Miss Shelby Gibbs.

By-Laws—Mrs. S. A. Montgomery, Mrs. Crow Girard, Mrs. J. E. Walker, Mrs. A. P. Holt, Mrs. E. G. Sewell, Mrs. C. P. Grey, Mrs. J. G. Snelling, Mrs. Joe Brown, Mrs. T. S. Randle, Mrs. W. M. Moreland, Mrs. M. N. James, Mrs. H. I. Lawrence.

Parsonage—Mrs. R. W. Vaughan, Mrs. Crow Girard, Mrs. Albert Lutz, Mrs. Will Lewis, Mrs. M. L. James.

Extension of Work—Mrs. A. P. Holt, Mrs. H. H. Hawsey, Mrs. James Brobson, Mrs. W. S. Middlemas, Mrs. Julia Robison, Mrs. W. J. Roach, Mrs. J. T. Butler, Mrs. E. J. Shaw, Mrs. A. F. Godat, Mrs. R. R. Lyons, Miss L. M. Mims, Miss Mary Werlein.

Bible study led by Miss Bennett; the central thought "Service through surrender," learned only through diligent study of God's word and prayer. The hymn, "Lead on, O King, Eternal," was an inspiration to all workers. After prayer and benediction by Rev. R. H. Wynn, the meeting adjourned.

THURSDAY AFTERNOON.

Devotional service led by Rev. R. H. Wynn. Minutes of morning session read and approved. In the absence of Mrs. Briscoe Carter, the report of Young People's Work was read by Mrs. Montgomery and accepted by the conference. Mrs. E. G. Sewell, Secretary Alexandria District, proved faithful work through her report. Delegates from the following auxiliaries gave items of interest in the work to the conference:

First Church, Rayne Memorial, Second Church, Carrollton, of New Orleans; First Church, Noel Memorial, of Shreveport; Opelousas, Natchitoches, Ruston, Arcadia, Minden, Gilbert and Lake Charles.

Mrs. A. P. Holt, delegate to the late Missionary Council, gave an interesting report of the sessions of that body, in recognition of which a rising vote of thanks was tendered her. After the Doxology and benediction the meeting adjourned.

FRIDAY MORNING.

The second day's session of the Home Department convened at 9 o'clock. Mrs. M. N. James conducted the devotional exercises. Hymn No. 351, "I Am Coming to the Cross," was the hymn used, and Mrs. James told us something of her beautiful ministrations in her Master's service. Mrs. E. G. Sewell offered a prayer. Mrs. Girard sang a beautiful solo.

Rev. George Jackson made a short talk to the conference. Mrs. Sewell gave a loving greeting from a little friend who is a missionary in darkest Africa.

The Secretary called the roll and read the minutes of the first day's session. The minutes were approved. The Corresponding Secretary read the report of the First Vice-President, Mrs. F. E. Russ. It was accepted by vote of the conference.

Mrs. R. H. Wynn, Second Vice-President, made her report, and it was accepted.

The Corresponding Secretary made the report for the third department, which was accepted.

Reports were read and accepted from the secretaries of the following districts: Monroe, Baton Rouge, Alexandria and Ruston. The Corresponding Secretary reported for the Lafayette, Shreveport and New Orleans Districts.

The following auxiliaries reported: Alexandria, Boyce, Jena, Columbia, Natchitoches, Kentwood, Wilson, Crowley, Lafayette, Lake Charles, Rayne, Oak Ridge, Gilbert, Girard, Rayville, Mer Rouge, Mary Werlein Mission, Rayne Memorial, Carrollton Avenue, First Church, New Orleans. The remaining reports from auxiliaries were deferred till the afternoon session.

Mrs. R. E. Bobbit read a suggestive and interesting paper on "How to Interest Young People in Missions."

The following resolution was adopted by a rising vote of the conference:

"Resolved, that since Mrs. Crow Girard, our efficient Corresponding Secretary, finds it imperative to give up her work, we extend to her our sincerest appreciation for her faithful and untiring service and pray that she may soon be able to return to the work.

"MRS. S. A. MONTGOMERY.
"MRS. R. W. VAUGHAN."

Rev. William Schuhle, Rev. H. R. Singleton, Rev. A. S. Lutz, Rev. N. E. Joyner, Rev. George Jackson and Rev. A. I. Townsley were presented to the body.

The hour having come, Brother Joyner began the Bible study by raising the tune of "Come Thou Fount of Every Blessing," in the good, old-fashioned way. The subject of his talk was: "The Kingdom of God." He read for a lesson those beautiful and blessed sayings of our Lord commonly called "The Beatitudes." The Sermon on the Mount was shown to be the rejoicing of a father who is bringing down to his children something to satisfy and fulfill every longing and desire of human heart. A motion prevailed that the regular order of business be suspended till 3 o'clock, so that the committees might have time to complete their work. Announcements were made and Brother Joyner pronounced the benediction.

AFTERNOON SESSION.

Mrs. J. M. Munholland led the devotional exercises, selecting the second chapter of Philippians for the scripture lesson. Rev. H. R. Singleton led in prayer. Hymn No. 489, "He Leadeth Me," concluded the devotional.

The minutes of the morning session were read and approved.

Mrs. A. A. Bartels read the report of the New Orleans City Mission Board. The following resolution was read by Mrs. J. G. Snelling:

"Resolved, That beginning with this conference we elect one District Secretary from each district, who shall represent the united work; that we elect one Conference Treasurer, who shall receive and disburse the funds of both departments.

"MRS. J. G. SNELLING.
"MRS. T. S. RANDLE.
"MISS MATTIE HOLT.
"MRS. J. W. JOHNSON.
"MRS. A. F. GODAT.
"MRS. W. J. ROACH.
"MRS. J. E. WALTER.

It was adopted, with the following addition: "keeping a separate bank account for each department."

Mrs. Girard brought Master A. I. Townsley, Jr., forward and presented him to the body. It was the pleasure of the conference to make this handsome boy a life member of the society. May his father's mantle fall on him!

Little Cassie Lavinia McDonald was also made a life member.

Reports from auxiliaries were resumed and the following heard from: Arcadia, Homer, Ruston, Minden, Mansfield, First Church, Shreveport; Noel Memorial, Shreveport, Winnfield and Monroe.

The Corresponding Secretary was instructed to wire a greeting to our Honorary Life President, Mrs. F. A. Lyons, and our former First Vice-President, Mrs. J. H. Reville, who are both ill.

Rev. J. N. H. Wharton, pastor of the Monroe Baptist Church, was presented and spoke a few words of felicitation to the body.

The report of the Committee on Parsonages was adopted.

Mrs. A. P. Holt read the report of the Committee on Extension of Work. The report was adopted as amended.

The Committee on By-Laws reported and the report was adopted.

The President announced the Nominating Committee, as follows: Mrs. W. W. Carre, New Orleans; Miss Hattie Renfro, Shreveport; Mrs. R. W. Vaughan, Ruston; Mrs. M. N. James, Boyce; Mrs. R. C. Holt, Rayne; Mrs. J. M. Munholland, Monroe; Miss Fannie Reams, Kentwood.

Rev. William Schuhle pronounced the benediction.

MRS. E. R. KENNEDY,

President.

MRS. H. R. SINGLETON,

Recording Secretary.

SATURDAY MORNING.

The meeting opened with singing "My Faith Looks Up to Thee." Mrs. J. C. Allen read the 91st Psalm, stressing its precious promises. Prayer by Mrs. McKinney. Minutes read and approved. The report of the Publication Committee, read by Mrs. McKinney, was accepted after slight change. A motion to make Miss Head a member of the conference, with full privileges, was unanimously carried. Mrs. Singleton moved 1000 copies of the minutes be printed; carried. It was moved and seconded Mrs.

M. E. Carr be given the rights of the floor. Mrs. Kennedy moved a rising vote of thanks be, tendered Mrs. Carr for past services in the work; carried. A review of the "Days of June" and "Kim Lu Bang," by Miss Mims and Mrs. Montgomery proved so forcible that many copies were sold. Miss Head talked on the reading course and mission study, urging special attention to the prescribed course and suggested a poster be placed in each auxiliary, "The Lord is well pleased with prompt and accurate reports."

The noon hour arrived. Miss Head conducted the service, her subject, "Fellowship with Christ Through Sacrifice," making his work a joy, giving instances of the power of definite, purposeful prayer and recommended close study of the reading course. After benediction by Rev. T. S. Randle adjournment was in order.

SATURDAY AFTERNOON.

The session met at 2:30 o'clock and opened with devotional service led by Mrs. D. C. Worrell. Minutes read and approved. The call for report on Young People's Work was given by Miss Ragland, item by item, and accepted after amendment by Mrs. Montgomery. The Finance Committee reported, through Mrs. R. C. Holt. Adopted. The Committee on Standing Rules reported, through Mrs. Montgomery. It was accepted after amendment. The claim on the Ring Scholarship was presented by Mrs. Montgomery and the payment partly met.

Visiting preachers to the conference were Revs. A. S. Lutz, Briscoe Carter, H. R. Singleton, Dr. S. S. Keener, R. W. Vaughan, Paul M. Brown, Rev. George Jackson, A. I. Townsley, Rev. R. H. Wynn, with the pastors of the Presbyterian and Baptist Churches.

Eighty delegates and visitors added largely to the interest of the meeting.

Invitations for place of next meeting were in order, Natchitoches was chosen.

After prayer for Divine guidance, balloting for officers for the united society was held, resulting in the election of Mrs. E. R. Kennedy, President; Mrs. J. G. Snelling, First Vice-President; Mrs. R. E. Bobbit, Second Vice-President; Mrs. R. H. Wynn, Third Vice-President; Mrs. S. A. Montgomery, Fourth Vice-President; Mrs. A. P. Holt, Corresponding Secretary of Foreign Department; Mrs. H. R. Singleton, Corresponding Secretary of Home Department; Mrs. J. J. Holmes, Treasurer; Mrs. D. C. Worrell, Recording Secretary; alternate to council meeting, Foreign Department, Mrs. J. J. Holmes. Alternate Home Department, Mrs. E. R. Kennedy. Superintendent of Press Work, Mrs. A. C. McKinney.

District Secretaries—Alexandria, Mrs. M. N. James; Baton Rouge, Mrs. B. E. Eskridge; Monroe, Mrs. S. S. Keener; Lafayette, Mrs. R. C. Holt; New Orleans, Mrs. Allen Godat; Ruston, Mrs. Will McKenzie; Shreveport, Mrs. U. L. Millsaps.

The election closing the business of the conference, adjournment was in order.　　　　MRS. W. W. CARRE,
　　　　　　　　　　　　　　　　　　　　President.
　　　　　　　　　MRS. A. A. BARTELS,
　　　　　　　　　　　　Recording Secretary.

PRESIDENT'S MESSAGE
HOME DEPARTMENT

Friends and Co-Workers:

We have looked forward with pleasant anticipation to this 19th annual meeting in Monroe. This city is my birthplace and has, naturally, many tender associations. We are glad to be with you, and as we pass on to the work of another year we look back with gratitude and forward with hope.

I want to thank this body for their co-operation and Christian fellowship, and to say that these years of service have been filled with blessings. The rough places have been smoothed and made level and beautiful by your love and sympathy and the guiding hand and presence of our Lord.

Some changes are always involved in progress, and we are now confronting, to some extent, a new order in our woman's work. We meet to-day, for the first time, a united body of Christian workers in one great Missionary Society—one in everything that tends to spread the love of Christ in human hearts and the rule of Christ in human society. By order of the General Conference of 1910 the Woman's Home Mission Society ceased to exist as a separate organization, and a brief review of its record may be of interest at this time. With a woman as its founder, it seems only natural that home building should be the foundation of the society. Without literature, without organizaiton, without leaders, with little or no co-operation on the part of the women of the Church, the little seed was planted in 1886 by Miss Lucinda Helm of Kentucky. It was called the "Woman's Department of Church Extension," endorsed by the authority of the Church. The seed sprouted and grew. At the close of the first quadrennium 7000 women had joined forces in this movement and ninety parsonages had been aided. We named the trunk of our tree "Parsonage Building," and its first branch, "Supplies." Since that time 2700 parsonages have been aided, to the amount of $280,000.

Goods valued at $200,000, sent to ministers in the hard places, to mission schools and orphanages, have given proof of the value of this tree and its first branch. Later the educational limb began to grow, by the establishment of two schools in Tampa, Florida. This part has grown into eleven educational centers, with a pupilage of nearly 1600 students. The uplift in the lives of these young people cannot be estimated. If there is one feature more important than another, it has come through the agency of that noble woman, Mrs. W. H. Johnson, of Dallas, Texas. She has helped to transform the lives of 1200 young girls from lives of sin into lives of honest, useful purpose. Twelve hundred girls, most of them under 20 years of age, motherless, homeless, friendless, given back hope and home and friends and God's love in their hearts. Some one said to Phillips Brooks: "To me you reveal more of God than any one else. I never think of you without soon forgetting you and thinking of God."

Mrs. Johnson's work appeals to me like that. We have dubbed other branches of this tree: "City Missions," "Deaconesses," "Local Work," "Tithing" and "Immigrant Work." Kindergartens, night schools, industrial schools, mothers' clubs and free reading rooms represent the active work of thirty city mission boards, including 96 salaried workers and 513 volunteer workers.

In seven years sixty-six deaconesses have been set apart for service and twenty more are to be consecrated during the session of the Missionary Council in St. Louis, besides nine city missionaries.

These women give themselves wholly to God's service by serving others. In the mills and mining camps, in the slums of the great cities, into the homes of poverty and sorrow, these messengers of Christ come with their healing, loving ministry. Through the three centers, located in Galveston, Texas; Gulfport, Miss., and New Orleans, thousands of strangers landing upon our shores have been reached and helped to better citizenship and higher ideals. Isaiah's prophecy, uttered 2500 years ago, is being realized in America to-day: "And all nations shall flow into it." This short review would be incomplete without mention of "Our Homes" and its beloved editor, Miss Mary Helm. This little white-winged messenger has done more, perhaps, to prepare the soil for our great Home Mission Tree than almost any other agency. It has gone into the homes of our people with its tidings of love and calls to service, conditions and needs have been presented with such convincing power that the great mother hearts of our women were touched and responses came in overflowing measure. Its career has closed with this record: Twenty-four thousand subscribers, $11,000, paid into the general treasury in eleven years, above all expenses, and without a single word of advertisement.

And now, dear friends, with this record of the past, shall we not go forward with greater zeal and more loyal service, as the united work opens up broader fields of opportunity and usefulness? Our work in Louisiana has prospered. During the last five years we have aided parsonages to the amount of $3000 from our half of dues, besides contributing to the general funds of the society. During this time we have raised, locally, nearly $40,000.

Considering the large Catholic element in Southern Louisiana, the scattered population in the lumber districts and the general failure of crops throughout the State for several years, we feel that God's guiding hand has been upon this work, and while we have planted, he alone has given the increase. The broad touch of human sympathy brings great results, and we are looking forward to the time when this great Missionary Society, united in prayer and faith and work, will touch other lives in even widening circles of influence, until "the earth shall be filled with the knowledge of the glory of the Lord, as the waters cover the sea." (Hab. 2-14.)

MRS. E. R. KENNEDY.

PRESIDENT'S MESSAGE
FOREIGN DEPARTMENT
(Thirty-two Years Young.)

This marks the thirty-second anniversary of the birth of the Woman's Foreign Missionary Society of the Louisiana Conference. It has been a busy one in all departments of missionary work, especially in the Foreign. The minds and hearts of Christian men and women are turning to the Orient, and with Christlike responsiveness are listening to the cry: "Come over and help us." So, as we meet in this beautiful church (the same that entertained us so delightfully two years ago) to celebrate the thirty-second birthday of our conference, may we pledge ourselves to the unswerving call of our Lord and say in answer: "What wilt thou have me to do." Then in loving obedience follow where he leads.

Yes, our dear society is thirty-two years young to-day, for we feel that we are yet children, with many things to learn and great things to do for our Master. Yet, when we recall the wonderful achievements our Lord wrought in that short space of time, we must acknowledge, with regret, our unworthiness as Methodist women of Louisiana, and that we have done so little in comparison to what we should have done. Most of our Lord's life was spent in preparation, silent years, of which we know so little; yet no one doubts the heart throbs, the anguish of soul he felt for a lost world, spending days and nights pleading with the Father for us.

Have we, dear sisters, at a conference spent the last three decades in a similar manner? If the past has been spent in this kind of preparation, then we are ready to begin real work—

17

then, indeed, this thirty-second anniversary would be an eventful one.

We have great cause for rejoicing, and with grateful hearts we acknowledge the continued goodness of the Father and his care and blessing on our work. My first interest in Foreign Mission work was thirty-eight years ago, when the Central Mexican Mission was formed. This was several years before the Woman's Board had an existence. However, we did not claim to be an independent association, but adopted the relation, as the Woman's Foreign Mission Society, auxiliary to the Board of Missions. This relation we maintained until we turned over our school in Mexico to the Woman's Board, which we did with the approval and consent of our dear Bishop and Mrs. Keener. The work in Mexico has been specially dear to me, and the members of the Carondelet, now First Church Society, in New Orleans.

Though the report of our Treasurer does not show the financial increase we had hoped and prayed for, yet the receipts are the largest we have ever had. The splendid report of our Corresponding Secretary shows an improvement in the number of auxiliaries and members. The opportunities for missionary work have never been more numerous or more important, so our responsibility is increased. May we heed the call that comes to us from China, from Korea, from Mexico and Brazil, from Cuba and other lands. May we listen to the voice of God as He calls us to do our share in the salvation of the world; and may our work be enlarged and our hearts open to respond to the larger demands made upon us by the unification of the Foreign and Home Mission Societies.

To be the right kind of a Christian one must be missionary in spirit—and I pray that this meeting may bring us closer to God and may we pledge ourselves to a renewed effort in all lines of work planned and recommended by our Missionary Council and the Mission Board.

MRS. W. W. CARRE.

REPORT OF CONFERENCE FIRST VICE-PRESIDENT.

It is with a feeling of deep gratitude and thankfulness to our Heavenly Father for his care and guidance that I submit this report to you. I think I may truly say that, in a general way, we have every reason to feel encouraged. "The Lord hath done great things for us; whereof we are glad."

I regret that I have not accomplished more, yet in my weakness I have tried to be of some service. The building of parsonages holds a peculiar interest for the membership, as well as the aid rendered the ministry.

The grants this year to parsonages by our conference society have been quite liberal:

To Hammond, for district parsonage, Baton
   Rouge District $300.00
To Winnfield, Ruston District.............. 100.00
To Wilson, Baton Rouge District........... 75.00
Slidell, New Orleans District................. 250.00
                                    ———
   Total $725.00

Many parsonages have been helped through the auxiliaries, but I have failed to receive the amounts.

It is always a source of disappointment not to know exactly what is being accomplished.

For local work the auxiliaries have expended $10,048.88. Through this local work the pastors can find an organized force ready to carry forward the best interests of the churches.

If the Woman's Home Mission Society is to be made the power for good that it can be, we must have mission study classes organized in every adult auxiliary. Interest comes from information.

Mrs. J. E. Leith, First Vice-President, Missionary Council, says: "Until there is an organization for the training of children in every church in the whole of Southern Methodism we have not done our full duty." Mrs. J. E. Grubbs, Second Vice-President, also stated: "If we would conserve the young people of Methodism to the missionary enterprise, they must be enlisted to-day, not to-morrow."

The outlook for the coming year is very hopeful, so let us go forward with greater energy and a renewed enthusiasm, a united band with faith in God, working to win

"Our country for Christ."

We can do it, if we will; but rather let us say, "We can do it—and we will."　　　　Respectfully submitted,

　　　　　　　　　MRS. FLORENCE E. RUSS.

———————

REPORT OF SECOND VICE-PRESIDENT.

I regret I am unable to report progress in this department. From the figures which I present it looks as if the work had gone backward. As soon after my appointment to the office as I could get the names of auxiliary officers I sent ninety-one circular letters, urging every woman in the important position of second vice-president to magnify her office. During the year I have heard from only eight auxiliaries in all, Boyce and Crowley showing the most active and intelligent interest in the conference. These auxiliaries seem to be emphasizing the scriptural method most strenuously, with the result that they are about the only ones who show any increase in the number of tithers reported.

Of course it is readily seen that the numbers sent to me cannot represent the full number of tithers in our churches, for the total number reported this year (69) is less than the increase last year over the previous one (89). This report is really so meager as to be almost worthless.

One hundred circular letters were sent out March 15 to the different pastors in our conference, requesting them to preach on the subject of Christian stewardship on a certain Sabbath.

Six personal letters were written, 348 leaflets and nine booklets, 106 report blanks and 149 pledge cards were mailed.

Reports were received as follows:

Alexandria District—
　　Boyce .·. ....　　11
Lafayette District—
　　Crowley ....　　19
Monroe District—
　　Monroe .. ..
　　Oak Ridge ....
Ruston District—
　　Ruston ....　　11
　　Haynesville .. ..　　12

WOMAN'S. MISSIONARY SOCIETY

New Orleans District—
    Carrollton Avenue 8
                                              —

    Total 69

No reports from Shreveport and Baton Rouge Districts during the year.   Respectfully submitted,

MRS. R. H. WYNN,

Second Vice-President.

REPORT OF THIRD VICE- PRESIDENT.

Number of Brigades, 23; number of members, 603; number on Baby Roll, 218; total money received from Brigade and Baby Roll, $169.64. The names of two babies were added to the list of life members: James Henry III of New Orleans and Eleanor Johnson of Mansfield.

REPORT OF CONFERENCE CORRESPONDING SECRETARY—HOME DEPARTMENT.

My Dear Friends: As we come before you to-day to give the record of the Home Mission work for the year which closed March 1, 1911, the feeling in our heart is one of mingled gratitude and sorrow. We must acknowledge that deep down in our heart is a longing for the old order, and we are loath to part with methods which have been so successful in the past. The year has been full of unrest, hesitation and uncertainty. We realize that the "Crisis hour in Missions" has been reached, and the bigness and grandeur of the outlook is appalling.

But while we stand at the threshold, viewing with our dull, human vision the enormity of this combined work, totally unable to pierce the veil of the future, still we go forward earnestly, willingly, yes, joyfully, because our Lord is leading, and it is His voice bidding us onward.

Oh, friends, what can we not attempt for such a leader? As we follow Christ the way opens up so beautifully and life means so much more and service becomes such a joy—even the hardest, roughest, stoniest places become altars of blessing, because just there the Savior came nearest to us, His loving arms were pressed closer about us, and His voice whispered in our ear: "Lo, I am with you." Oh, the unmeasured, hallowed joy in the presence of such a Savior! Let us, as a united body of Christian women, press forward to greater effort, and conquer in His name.

During the year just closed our membership has increased about three hundred, until now we number nearly 2800 members. Nine new auxiliaries have been organized, as follows:

Houma and Sulphur, in the Lafayette District.
Bienville and Athens—Ruston District.
Rochelle and Oak Grove—Alexandria District.
Girard and Rayville—Monroe District.
New Roads—Baton Rouge District.

Parsonages have been helped to the amount of $725.00. By resolution of the Woman's Missionary Council the privilege has been given to us of aiding parsonages for one year longer, for which we rejoice, as this work is much needed in our conference. By the end of this year we expect the Conference Board of Church Extension to be in a position to handle the parsonage work, as one-fifth of the whole assessment for church extension is to be appropriated to the aid of parsonages.

During the month of February a circular letter was sent to each auxiliary, asking that they pledge a certain amount over and above dues for the extension of our work, the maintenance of the schools and missions already established by the Board, the support of missionaries, deaconesses, etc., etc. Only a small per cent. of the auxiliaries replied, but we trust that this work will be remembered and the money sent to the Treasurer.

At the annual meeting held in New Orleans a year ago the Corresponding Secretary was instructed to get definite information from Mrs. MacDonell in regard to certain reports of local work. The answer received concerning visits to sick and strangers is as follows:

"That a visitor who calls on twenty different women in the same house, going into their different rooms, even though in the house, it certainly would be twenty visits. We reckon this as a physician would do. If he went to call at a flat, where he went into six different apartments, he would enter it on his books as six visits. If, however, he should find them all in one room he would enter it as one visit. I think the same obtains in our social service."

About 800 letters, postals, etc., have been sent out by your Secretary. Also 750 annual reports, 150 Board reports and several thousand leaflets, booklets, helps, organization blanks, etc.

We are deeply grateful to our Father for His tender care and the progress of our loved work. Interest has grown, and the sentiment among our people over the State is very strong for missions. Letters of inquiry concerning different phases of the work show an intelligent grasp of things and a more enlarged vision.

The following is the statistical report for the year, March 1, 1910, to March 1, 1911:

		Increase.
Number adult auxiliaries	84	5
Number adult members	2090	150
Number young people's and juvenile auxiliaries	5	1
Number young people's and juvenile members	61	7
Total members	2773	279
Number life members	41	..
Number added to Baby Roll	262	..
Number members Brigade	622	122
Number subscribers to "Voice"	472	..
Number Home Mission Reading Course	70	..
Number Tithing	293	137
Number boxes sent off	17	..
Number papers and leaflets sent	7541	..
Number auxiliaries observing Week of Prayer	34	..
Number visits to sick, etc	8207	..
Number visits to institutions	752	..
Number cottage prayer meetings	144	..
Number garments	5338	..
Number needy assisted	32	..
How many aux. hold union meetings?	8	
How many aux. represented in City M. B.	9	
Amount sent Con. Treas. for dues	$1689.43	..
Amount sent Con. Treas. for specials	1063.00	..
Total for connectional	2752.00	..
Amount for local work	10,980.00	..

Life members: Eleanor Johnson, Mansfield; James Henry III, New Orleans.

MRS. CROW GIRARD.

FIRST ANNUAL MEETING

ANNUAL REPORT OF CONFERENCE CORRESPONDING SECRETARY.

FOREIGN DEPARTMENT.

		Gain.
Districts	7	..
Adult Auxiliaries	35	..
Adult New Auxiliaries	2	..
Adult Members	987	69
Adult New Members	123	..
Young People's Societies	3	1
New Young People's Societies	1	..
Young People Members	63	41
New Young People Members	38	..
Juvenile Societies	11	1
New Juvenile Societies	..	..
Juvenile Members	230	107
New Juvenile Members	63	..
Total Members	1280	83
Life Members	29	3
Honorary Members	41	..
Honorary Life Members	1	..
Honorary Life Patrons	1	..
Subscribers to Missionary Voice	301	..
Subscribers to Young Christian Worker	193	..
Scholarships	18	..
Bible Women	7	
Study Circles	11	..
Members in Study Circles	240	..

With grateful hearts we review the records of the past year, for we note an increase in membership and the largest amount of money ever paid into the treasury. We did not reach the two thousand dollars promised on the Conference Pledge by $227.21, and we lacked $17.76 of paying the $100.00 pledged on the Missionary Retirement Fund. Possibly we set our mark too high, but it is better to aim high and fall short of the mark than to always keep our eyes upon the ground. Let us not be satisfied unless each year notes a marked advance over the preceding one.

Two hundred and twenty-four new members have been added to the roll during the year, and yet the net increase is only eighty-three, showing that we either do not hold the new members or that the auxiliary corresponding secretaries are remiss about making accurate reports. I'm sure much of the blame lies at the latter point, as some auxiliaries do not send reports regularly.

One missing link effects the whole chain, from auxiliary to district, from district to conference, from conference to council, and from council to Board of Missions. Upon you, then, auxiliary corresponding secretaries, rests the responsibility of correct reports.

The auxiliaries have been supplied with 4345 copies of choice leaflets, 300 summaries of the last Board report, 53 hand-books, 500 copies of the conference minutes, 150 copies of the Board report and 240 circular letters by the corresponding secretary.

The Missionary Voice has a subscription list of only 301 and the Young Christian Worker 193, out of a membership of 1280. This is a reflection upon the intelligence and interest of our women which, I trust, we will not let stand any longer. Now that this magazine is the combination of our three missionary organs (and can be had for the price of one), we should have a subscription list at least commensurate with our combined membership.

Only two new auxiliaries have been organized during the year, one adult and one young people, at Gibsland. You might ask your district secretaries why this small increase.

The standard of the "Roll of Honor" having been raised at our last annual meeting, only one auxilary (Baton Rouge) has attained the goal—or if they have they have not so reported.

The conference is supporting eighteen scholarships in foreign fields and one in the Scarritt Bible and Training School, seven Bible women and two missionaries. Miss Ada Parker has temporarily resigned on account of the death of her mother and the feeble health of her father. We assure her of our loving sympathy in her bereavement and pray that other hands may be led to take up the work she has so reluctantly laid aside.

We note an increase in the number of study circles reported this year. Last year only three were reported. This year there are eleven, with 240 members. Not until our women read and study will they be deeply in earnest about missionary effort. If you have not read the book for the study course this year ("Western Women in Eastern Lands") you have not entered into the spirit of the Jubilee celebration of woman's work for missions.

A splendid series of national jubilee meetings are being held, in the interest of Foreign Missions and large contributions of money have been made for the extension of the kingdom, to say nothing of the widening of the spiritual vision of those who have participated in these meetings. The women of Southern Methodism have been asked to contribute $50,000.00 as a jubilee gift to erect a building for our girls' school in Rio de Janeiro, Brazil. How much of this amount will the Louisiana Conference contribute? Only one auxiliary in the conference, so far as I know, has held a jubilee meeting, and that is our youngest organization—Natchitoches. I may say in behalf of New Orleans that we were planning for a meeting there but were requested by the central committee to wait until fall as they were planning a series of meetings to be held in large cities at that time and New Orleans was included in the number. We trust other meetings will be held throughout the conference and that $1000.00 may be raised on this jubilee offering. The day of small things is past in the extension of God's kingdom. If we would measure up to our responsibility and privilege in this age of the world's advancement we must undertake greater things for him. The heathen world is challenging us to-day to live up to what we profess to believe and be. Shall we not accept the challenge? Or will we disappoint them and our Heavenly Father who is depending upon us to take or send the gospel to the uttermost parts of the earth?

For several years the tendency has been toward the union of our missionary forces in the Church, and this year marks the consummation of those plans. With a tinge of sadness we close the records and lay down the old plan, but with a note of joy and hope for a larger work we take up the new. May no discordant note be heard in this united family, but with every shoulder to the wheel let us heed the command of the leader of our ranks and "Go Forward," presenting a solid front against the enemy, and in his strength conquer the world for Christ.

MRS. S. A. MONTGOMERY.

REPORT CITY MISSION BOARD—NEW ORLEANS.

The Woman's Board of City Missions is composed of sixty-three delegates, representing nine home mission societies, and

an advisory board consisting of the presiding elder and the pas·
tors in charge of the various churches in the city. Representation on the Board is not graded by membership in the auxiliary,
but each society affiliating with the Board is entitled to six delegates besides the wife of the pastor, who is a member ex-officio.
. . During the year the Board held fifteen meetings—eleven regular, two executive, one parlor conference and one reception.

The Board has headquarters at St. Mark's Hall, where a
superintendent and two deaconesses are in charge, and also con-·
ducts mission work uptown, with the Werlein Mission as a
center and a city missionary in charge. · Their work is·supple-
mented in a small degree by the service of volunteers.

In April the Board prepared two memorials—one to the
General Board, asking that the office of corresponding secretary
be created for city mission boards. It received favorable action.
The other, to the General Conference, prayed that the rights
of laity might be granted the women of Southern Methodism.
It was not granted.

In May the Board entertained the Woman's Home Mission
Society of the Louisiana Conference at their annual meeting and
received an inspiration and an uplift at this most successful meet-·
ing.

In January a parlor conference of mission workers was
called by the President and held in her home. It was largely
attended and plans for maintaining and extending the work were
discussed. The plan adopted was to make an effort to get 2000
members at $1.00 a year, thereby securing an annual income of
$2000 to carry on the work.

Recently, by permission of the Board, the Free Kindergarten
Association opened a school in St. Mark's Hall and daily conducted an up-to-date kindergarten for the young children of the
neighborhood.

I do not wish to trespass upon the reports of the deaconesses
or the City Missionary, but this report would be incomplete did
it not in some way recognize the faithful and efficient work of
these women, who daily "tread the crowded ways of life," bringing comfort and hope, love and good cheer to many weary hearts.
Of the sewing school, under Miss Ragland; the cooking school,

under Miss Baker; the clinic, the boys and girls' clubs, the baths, the visits to the poor and needy, the rescue of the perishing, the tender ministrations to the dying, etc., will be told in detail in their reports.

The Board counts itself most fortunate in having for superintendent so zealous and efficient a man as Mr. N. E. Joyner.

The Board is indebted to Dr. Gertrude Wilcox, a practicing physician, who, without compensation, conducts for them a clinic for girls and women at St. Mark's Hall.

While the backward glance shows a steady progress, it tells but little of the hard work and frequent discouragement. We women who do Home Mission work are like the tapestry weavers of old, who wrought steadily on the underside, weaving their loops in their work but not knowing until their labor was ended how well they had wrought. So we must learn that the Master hand which has drawn our pattern, planned the dark places as well as the bright ones to complete the design. Then when our work is over, may it be given to us to view with Him, the finished pattern from the other side, and hear at the last His "well done, good and faithful servant."

(MRS. JOHN B.) HATTIE R. PARKER,
Corresponding Secretary.

REPORT OF CITY MISSIONARY—NEW ORLEANS.

Number of visits, 874; visits to institutions, 149; papers and tracts given out, 260; Bibles, 8; Testaments, 5; copies of gospels, 8; opportunities for prayer and Bible reading, 281; number of persons aided, $2.50; groceries given, 50 times; amount spent for various needs of poor, $175.75; amount spent for medicine for sick, $16.90; amount given in cash, $31.50; children placed in asylums, 7; other homes secured, 4; cases placed in hospitals, 3; amount collected for invalids' rent, $33.00.

L. MEEKINS.

WOMAN'S MISSIONARY SOCIETY

REPORT OF TREASURER—HOME DEPARTMENT.

RECEIPTS.

Received for Dues	$1,689.43
Received for Life Membership	20.00
Received for Baby Roll	23.74
Received for Week of Prayer.....................	412.88
Received for Mite Boxes	107.23
Received for Specials	4.00
Received for Brigade Dues	13.27
Received for Free Will Offering..................	94.75
Received for Collection New Orleans..............	57.90
Received for Conference Expense Fund...........	214.04
Received from General Treasurer for Expense Fund...	114.78
Balance on hand from 1910.......................	279.78
	$3,031.80
Total Disbursements	2,899.80
Balance on hand	$ 132.13
Scarritt Scholarship ....$	88.39
Deaconess Fund	18.15
Conference Expense Fund	25.59
	$ 132.13
Total by Voucher for 1910.......................	$ 9,925.62
Total by Voucher for 1911.......................	10,980.89
Net gain over 1910..........................	$ 1,055.27

(Grand total, 1910, $13,093.76; grand total, 1911, $13,732.91. Total net gain, $639.15.)

Parsonages aided—

Hammond ....$	300.00
Winnfield	100.00
Wilson	75.00
Total	$ 475.00

DISBURSEMENTS.

Amount to General Treasurer	$2,355.30
Amount to Mrs. McKinney to Annual Meeting.....	12.80
Amount to Mrs. A. E. Price to Annual Meeting......	1.25
Amount to Mrs. M. N. James to Annual Meeting....	12.50
Amount to Mrs. J. H. Reville to Annual Meeting.....	22.50
Amount to Mrs. J. N. Sandlin to Annual Meeting....	12.20
Amount to Mrs. R. C. Holt to Annual Meeting.......	9.60
Amount to Mrs. E. R. Kennedy to Annual Meeting..	8.60

Amount to Mrs. R. H. Singleton to Annual Meeting.. 11.60
Amount to Mrs. R. P. Amacker to Annual Meeting... 6.90
Amount to Mrs. Crow Girard to Annual Meeting.... 8.60
Amount to Mrs. J. H. Reville, Expenses Meeting..... 8.00
Expenses Mrs. Crow Girard, 1910 and 1911.:........ 73.59
Expenses Mrs. John Munholland 2.25
Expenses Mrs. Robert Wynn 4.01
Expenses Miss Fannie Reams.................... 2.77
Expenses Mrs. A. E. Price...................... 6.21
Expenses Mrs. M. N. James 26.34
Expenses Mrs. A. C. McKinney.................... 6.66
Expenses Mrs. J. H. Reville..................... 16.22
Expenses Mrs. J. N. Sandlin.................... 12.09
Expenses Mrs. John Munholland 7.17
Expenses Mrs. R. C. Holt 8.00
Expenses Mrs. Sexton in New Orleans............ 1.00
Expense Lafayette Advertiser 5.25
Expense Palfrey-Purcell, Printing Minutes.......... 120.25
Expense Scarritt Scholarship 100.00
Expense Mrs. R. W. McDonald 28.01
Expense Life Membership 10.00

Total Disbursements \$2,899.67

RECAPITULATION.

Total cash received this year.....................\$2,752.02
Total by Voucher 10,980,89

Grand Total \$13,732.91

MRS. R. C. HOLT.

MRS. CROW GIRARD,
Lafayette.

Dear Madam: After a careful and thorough examination of the Treasurer's books of the Woman's Home Mission Society, I am pleased to state that the accounts are correct.

Balance on hand March 15, 1910...................\$ 279.78
Amount received during the year 1910............. 2,752.02

\$3,031.80
Amount paid out 2,899.67

Balance on hand ....\$ 132.13

Respectfully,
MRS. ERNEST LEVY, Auditor.

ALEXANDRIA DISTRICT.

Auxiliary—	Dues	Baby Roll	Week of Prayer	Mite Boxes	Brigade Dues	Conference Expense and Contingent Fund	Specials	Totals	Amount by Voucher
Alexandria	$45.00		$10.50	$11.69	$.40	$5.00	$1.00	$57.50	$770.35
Boyce	27.90	$1.50	4.30					50.79	255.65
Tioga	4.05							4.05	125.00
Opelousas	6.20		10.00			.45	1.00	17.65	
Colfax	16.30	1.25						17.55	200.67
Jena	17.00		8.80			1.50		27.30	294.95
Quadrate	11.30	.25		1.60				13.15	53.20
Columbia	13.90							13.90	176.85
Eden	19.10		4.50	4.60	1.60	2.40	7.05	39.25	
Trout	30.65	.25		7.81		.75		39.46	19.25
Natchitoches	14.40		18.85	18.42	9.40		5.00	57.07	10.25
Melville	16.15							16.15	
Lecompte	24.20		13.75					37.95	58.70
Rochelle	7.70							7.70	3.25
Hamilton	2.50			2.10	.90			5.50	
Total	$257.35	$3.25	$70.70	$46.22	$13.30	$10.10	$14.05	$404.97	$1,968.12

BATON ROUGE DISTRICT.

Auxiliary—	Dues	Baby Roll	Week of Prayer	Mite Boxes	Brigade Dues	Conference Expense and Contingent Fund	Specials	Totals	Amount by Voucher
St. Francisville	$ 11.65	......	$ 4.40	......	......	$ .20	$ 1.00	$ 17.25	$ 77.85
Baker	18.80	......	......	......	......	3.00	......	21.80	......
Amite	9.90	......	......	......	......	......	......	9.90	227.53
Wilson	37.30	......	5.00	......	......	7.20	......	49.50	52.60
Bogalusa	8.70	3.30	......	$ 4.71	......	......	......	16.71	......
Slaughter	......	......	......	......	......	2.70	......	2.70	......
Kentwood	24.45	......	4.30	......	......	......	......	28.75	11.13
Franklinton	20.60	......	......	......	......	......	......	20.60	29.50
Hammond	25.20	......	......	......	......	......	......	25.20	......
Ponchatoula	6.25	......	......	......	......	......	......	6.25	......
Totals	$162.85	$ 3.30	$13.70	$ 4.71	......	$13.10	$ 1.00	$198.66	$398.61

RUSTON DISTRICT.

Auxiliary—	Dues	Baby Roll	Week of Prayer	Mite Boxes	Brigade Dues	Conference Expense and Contingent Fund	Specials	Totals	Amount by Voucher
Ruston	$ 36.20		14.79			$ 7.80	$ 7.00	$ 65.79	$ 94.25
Minden	40.95		8.35	.70		6.60	14.00	70.60	41.85
Homer	25.50					3.45		28.95	574.35
Haynesville	19.40		8.00	4.20		1.20		32.80	35.00
Bernice	6.50							6.50	49.00
Winnfield	32.45					2.40		34.85	12.88
Benton	6.00					.20		6.20	
Spring Hill	6.20					2.30		8.50	55.95
Haughton	21.80			1.41				23.21	16.05
Totals	$195.00		$31.14	$ 6.31		$23.95	$21.00	$277.40	$879.33

SHREVEPORT DISTRICT.

Auxiliary—	Dues	Baby Roll	Week of Prayer	Mite Boxes	Brigade Dues	Conference Expense and Contingent Fund	Specials	Totals	Amount by Voucher
First Church	$142.40	......	$22.45	......	......	$ 5.00	......	$169.85	$1,349.52
Texas Avenue	18.40	.50	6.10	.50	......	1.35	3.00	29.85	1,159.51
Noel's Chapel	63.60	......	17.00	2.90	......	6.35	......	89.85	519.80
Leesville	66.30	3.00	18.50	4.65	......	7.25	8.00	107.70	55.98
Zwolle	18.40	......	......	......	......	......	......	18.40	157.45
Grand Cane	14.40	......	7.60	......	......	4.85	......	26.85	14.65
Logansport	17.80	4.00	1.50	......	.60	5.35	......	29.25	......
De Ridder	18.85	......	......	......	......	......	......	18.85	15.00
Provencal	2.90	......	......	......	......	......	......	2.90	......
Mansfield	32.30	......	19.60	......	......	5.00	10.00	66.90	560.30
Many	14.20	.75	......	2.59	......	3.00	.80	21.34	......
Keithville	11.20	......	4.00	......	......	......	......	15.20	20.75
Totals	$420.75	$ 8.25	$96.75	$10.64	$ .60	$38.15	$21.80	$596.94	$3,852.96

LAFAYETTE DISTRICT.

Auxiliary—	Dues	Baby Roll	Week of Prayer	Mite Boxes	Brigade Dues	Conference Expense and Contingent Fund	Specials	Totals	Amount by Voucher
Crowley	$ 27.30	$ .50	$ 6.60	$ 7.08	$ 1.00	$ 3.45	$14.00	$ 59.93	$ 410.65
Lake Charles	30.10	.....	2.50	2.00	.....	5.85	.....	40.45	145.75
Rayne	27.10	1.89	18.56	11.74	.....	2.50	5.30	67.09	25.70
Morgan City	9.60	.....	4.35	.....	.....	3.20	.....	17.15	114.05
Franklin	13.90	.....	.....	.....	.....	.45	.....	14.35	56.50
Eunice	25.55	.....	3.30	2.40	6.87	4.15	.....	42.27	21.50
St. Martinsville	3.90	.....	.....	.....	.....	.90	.....	4.80	.....
Houma	10.50	.....	.....	.....	.....	.....	.....	10.50	16.50
Lafayette	38.67	1.00	30.00	5.17	.80	10.70	21.00	107.34	390.71
Lake Arthur	3.40	.....	.....	.....	.....	.....	.....	3.40	.....
Totals	$190.02	$ 3.39	$65.31	$28.39	$ 8.67	$31.20	$40.30	$367.28	$1,181.36

MONROE DISTRICT.

Auxiliary—	Dues	Baby Roll	Week of Prayer	Mite Boxes	Brigade Dues	Conference Expense and Contingent Fund	Specials	Totals	Amount by Voucher
Mornoe	$ 53.20		$ 9.50			$23.75	$ 1.00	$ 87.45	$237.60
Mer Rouge	27.90	.75	17.00	4.20	$ .70	7.35		57.90	97.75
Oak Ridge	14.15	2.05		.24				16.44	10.00
Gilbert	14.75		2.25			2.25		19.25	25.65
Winnsboro	2.07							2.07	31.90
Waterproof	15.00		5.40			2.55		22.95	
West Monroe	8.00					18.35		26.35	19.50
Girard	9.00					2.25		11.25	
Totals	$144.07	$ 2.80	$34.15	$ 4.44	$ .70	$56.50	$ 1.00	$243.66	$422.40

Auxiliary—	Dues	Baby Roll	Week of Prayer	Mite Boxes	Brigade Dues	Conference Expense and Contingent Fund	Specials	Totals	Amount by Voucher
First Church	$ 69.40	$ .25	$17.20	$ .37		$11.68	$ .60	$ 99.50	$ 321.38
Rayne Memorial	55.20	....	11.00	....		12.61	....	78.81	706.35
Louisiana Avenue	34.60	....	7.55	....		....	....	42.15	506.12
Parker Memorial	28.35	....	....	....		4.65	....	33.00	154.15
Mary Werlein Mission	22.80	....	10.75	....		....	....	33.55	....
Algiers	16.10	....	9.65	....		2.75	....	28.50	116.02
Carrollton Avenue	31.70	1.00	20.00	....		3.95	3.00	59.65	292.54
Vacherie	12.30	1.50	18.50	3.85		3.00	7.00	46.15	40.53
Pearl River	10.20	....	2.05	1.30		....	....	13.55	17.22
Plaquemine	2.40	....	....	....		....	....	2.40	110.60
Second Church	18.00	....	2.83	....		....	....	20.83	....
Donaldsonville	7.60	....	1.60	....		....	....	9.20	5.70
Madisonville	4.00	....	....	....		....	....	4.00	....
Felicity	6.74	....	....	....		....	....	6.74	7.50
Totals	$319.39	$ 2.75	101.13	$ 5.52		$38.64	$10.60	$478.03	$2,278.11

REPORTS OF DISTRICT SECRETARIES.
HOME DEPARTMENT.
ALEXANDRIA DISTRICT.

		Inc.	Dec.
Number of Adult Auxiliaries	16	2	..
Number of Adult Members	298	22	..
Number of Brigades	7	4	..
Total number of Brigade members	165	81	...
Total number of members in district	463	187	..
Total number life members	2	..	..
Number of members on Baby Roll	42	..	13
Number of subscribers to Missionary Voice	107	4	..
Number taking Home Mission Reading Course	32.	12	..
Number using leaflets, bulletins and secular press	14	10	..
Number pledged to tithing	37	20	..
Number boxes of supplies sent off and reported to Supt. Supply Dept	6	1	..
Number of papers and leaflets distributed	1139	319	..
Number of Auxiliaries observing Week of Prayer	9	4	..
Number of visits made to sick and strangers	1380	343	..
Number of cottage prayer meetings or Bible readings held	..	..	8
Number of garments in good order distribut'd	362	..	259
Amount of money sent to Conference Treasurer for dues	$ 257.35	$27.04	..
Amount of money sent to Conference Treasurer for specials	108.62	..	..
Amount of money expended for local work	2224.47	222.01	...
Increase money sent Conference Treasurer	..	27.04	..
Increase local work	..	222.01	..
Letters written to Auxiliaries	100	8	..
Letters written to ministers	24	..	..
Letters written to Conference Officers	20	..	..
Postals written	30	..	..
Copies Ministers and Auxiliaries	120	..	..
Copies sent Ministers	25	..	..
Leaflets distributed	1800	..	..

MRS. M. N. JAMES, District Secretary.

FOREIGN DEPARTMENT.

		Inc.	Dec.
Number of Members	119	5	..
Number new Members	5	..	..
Life Members	6	..	..
Honorary Members	2	..	..
Subscribers to Missionary Voice	76	..	..

		Inc.	Dec.
Subscribers to Young Christian Worker.....	13	..	..
Scholalrships... ...	2	..	..
Dues	$93.00	..	..
Conference Expense Fund ...	33.00	..	..
Pledge ...	229	..	..
Scholarships—Robbie Foster $60, Korean $40	100	..	..
Specials—Retirement Fund ...	6	..	..
Total ...	463	..	..

MRS. E. G. SEWELL. District Secretary.

BATON ROUGE DISTRICT.

HOME DEPARTMENT.

		Inc.	Dec.
Number of Adult Auxiliaries...	11	..	..
Number of Adult members...	217	..	8
Number of Brigades...	2	..	..
Total number of Brigade members...	69	..	..
Total number of members in district...	286	..	8
Total number of life members...	1	..	..
Number of subscribers to "Our Homes"...	34	..	37
Number taking Home Mission Reading Course	1	..	..
Number using leaflets, bulletins and secular press	4	..	..
Number pledged to tithing...	9	4	..
Number of papers and leaflets distributed..	386	194	..
Number of Auxiliaries observing Week of Prayer	4	..	..
Number of visits made to sick and strangers	467	275	..
Number of garments in good order distributed	98	..	..
Amount of money sent to Conference Treasurer for dues ...$	117.25	..	$11.27
Amount of money sent to Conference Treasurer for specials ...	42.70	$30.20	..
Amount of money expended for local work—$1021.08		207.66	..

FANNYE REAMES, District Secretary.

FOREIGN DEPARTMENT.

		Inc.	Dec.
Number members ...	110	..	30
Subscribers to Missionary Voice...	38	..	..
Number life members ...	1	..	..
Subscribers to Young Christian Worker.....	15	..	..
Dues ...	$81.10	..	..
Conference Expense Fund ...	13.45	..	..
Pledge ...	108.46	..	..
Scholarships ...	120.00	..	..
Trueheart Lectureship ...	5.00	..	..
Retirement Fund ...	1.30	..	..
		..	..
Total ...	$329.51	..	..

MRS. B. E. ESKRIDGE, District Secretary.

LAFAYETTE DISTRICT.

HOME DEPARTMENT.

		Inc.	Dec.
Number of Auxiliaries in District...	10	..	..
Number of New Auxiliaries...	2	..	..

		Inc.	Dec.
Number of Adult Members	258	..	..
Number of Brigade Members	131	..	..
Number subscribers to Missionary Voice	94	..	..
Number Tithing	159	..	..
Number papers and leaflets distributed	808	..	..
Number boxes of supplies sent off	4	..	..
Total sent Conference Treasurer	$367.28	..	..
Local work	1181.36	..	..

MRS. A. E. PRICE, District Secretary.

FOREIGN DEPARTMENT.

		Inc.	Dec.
Nomber Members	167	21	..
New Members	21	..	..
Life Members	2	..	..
Honorary Members	7	..	..
Subscribers to "Missionary Voice"	41	..	..
Subscribers to Young Christian Worker	30	..	..
Scholarships	2	..	..
Dues	$120.12	..	..
Conference Expense Fund	16.60	..	..
Pledge	191.10	..	..
Thank Offering	59.10	..	..
Minutes	6.60	..	..
Scholarships	30.00	..	..
Mite Boxes	4.50	..	..
Retirement	9.10	..	..
Juvenile Kindergarten Pledge	12.96	..	..
Sewing Material	3.00	..	..
Total	$503.08	..	..
Members using Study Courses	68	..	..
Gain		65.22	

MRS. A. P. HOLT, District Secretary.

NEW ORLEANS DISTRICT.

HOME DEPARTMENT.

		Inc.	Dec.
Number of Adult Auxiliaries	16	2	..
Number of Adult Members	406	..	..
Total number of members in district	456	..	..
Total number of life members	14	1	..
Number of members on Baby Roll added during year	34	28	..
Number of members of Florine McEachern Mite Box Brigade	50	..	..
Number of subscribers The Missionary Voice	113	..	..
Number taking Home Mission Reading Course	15	..	..
Number pledged to tithing	43	..	..
Number boxes of supplies sent off and reported to Supt. Supply Dept	4	..	..
Number of papers and leaflets distributed	2514	..	..
Number of auxiliaries observing Week of Prayer	8	..	..
Number of visits made to sick and strangers	2307	..	..

Number of visits made to corrective or be-
nevolent institutions 368
Number of cottage prayer meetings or Bible
readings held 65
Number of garments in good order distrib-
uted, ($150.65) 2814
Number of needy assisted.................. 8
Do the auxiliaries in the district hold union
meetings? .... Yes.
Any Woman's Boards of City Missions in dis-
trict? .. .. Yes.
How many auxiliaries identified with them?.. 8
How many city missionaries are employed?. 2
Amount of money sent to Conference Treas.. $478.77
Amount of money expended for local work.. 2278.11
Amount sent C. M. Board.................. 690.90
Amount collected, Week of Prayer........... 89.97
Bouquets to sick 34
Bibles and Testaments given............... 9
Thanksgiving offering $75.00
Box to Orphanage Home................... 10.05

MRS. JOHN MUNFORD, District Secretary.

FOREIGN DEPARTMENT.

		Inc.	Dec.
Number Members	242	..	..
Life Members	14	..	..
Subscribers to Missionary Voice...........	67	..	..
Subscribers to Young Christian Worker......	11	..	..
Scholarships supported	5	..	..
Bible Women	3	..	..
Dues	$182.80	..	..
Conference Expense Fund	23.96	..	..
Pledge for missionaries' salaries..........	459.05	..	..
Retirement Fund	20.50	..	..
Bible Women	160.25	..	..
Scholarships	168.75	..	..
Mite Boxes	19.65	..	..
Special for furnishing room in Lucy Cun- ningham School	20.00	..	..
Special to China	100.00	..	..
For printing minutes	2.50	..	..
From buds and blossoms.................	.75	..	..
Total	$1158.21		
Adult Auxiliaries	7	..	..
Young People's Auxiliaries	1	..	..

MRS. D. C. WORRELL, District Secretary.

MONROE DISTRICT.

FOREIGN DEPARTMENT.

Number of Members	115	..	..
Number nwe members...................	51	..	..
Subscribers to "Missionary Voice"..........	14	..	..
Subscribers to Young Christian Worker......	20	..	..

FIRST ANNUAL MEETING

		Inc.	Dec.
Dues	$116.85	..	..
Conference Expense Fund	$17.35	..	..
Thank offering	10.00	..	..

MRS. S. S. KEENER, District Secretary.

RUSTON DISTRICT.

HOME DEPARTMENT.

		Inc.	Dec.
Number of Adult Auxiliaries...............	8	..	..
Number of Adult Members...................	190	..	..
Number subscribers to Missionary Voice...	59	..	..
Number pledged to tithing.................	18	..	..
Number boxes of supplies sent off and reported to Supt. Supply Dept............	3	..	..
Number of papers and leaflets distributed..	726	..	..
Number of auxiliaries observing Week of Prayer	1	..	..
Number of visits made to sick and strangers	1078	..	.
Number of cottage prayer meetings or Bible readings held.................	6	..	..
Number of garments in good order distribt'd.	184	..	..
Number of needy assisted.................	16	..	..
Amount of money sent to Conference Treas..	$195.00	..	..
Amount of money expended for local work..	617.65	..	..
Conference Expense Fund..................	6.95	...	..
Amount to Orphanage	77.40	..	..
Cash to needy	93.70	..	..
Extra dollar	7.00	..	..
Specials—Twenty-five dol. 20c.............	24.20	..	..
Value of boxes sent off...................	35.35	..	..
Collected in Mite Boxes..................	1.41	..	..
Honorary members	14	..	..
Auxiliaries organized	1	..	..

Total money collected...................$1007.41

MRS. A. C. McKINNEY, District Secretary.

FOREIGN DEPARTMENT.

		Inc.	Dec.
Number Members	176	..	..
New Members	16	..	..
Life Members	1	..	..
Honorary Members	7	..	..
Subscribers to "Missionary Voice"..........	56	..	..
Subscribers to Young Christian Worker......	21	..	..
Dues	$105.40	..	..
Conference Expense Fund	13.15	..	..
Pledge	134.95	..	..
Thank Offering	8.65	..	..
Scholarships	40.00	..	..
Specials	63.72	..	..
Total	377.87	..	..

MRS. B. F. DUDLEY, District Secretary.

WOMAN'S MISSIONARY SOCIETY

SHREVEPORT DISTRICT.

HOME DEPARTMENT.

		Inc.	Dec.
Number of Adult Auxiliaries	14	..	..
Number of Members	432	..	..
Number of Brigade Members	133	..	..
Total number of Members	481	..	..
Number of subscribers to "Missionary Voice"	148	..	..
Number of Tithers	53	..	..
Visits to sick and strangers	2159	..	..
Papers and leaflets distributed	1461	..	..
Boxes of supplies sent off	3	..	..
Amount of money sent Conference Treas	$596.94	..	..
Amount of money expended for local work	3852.96	..	..

MRS. A. J. PEEVY, District Secretary.

FOREIGN DEPARTMENT.

		Inc.	Dec.
Number of Members	219	19	..
Life Members	5	..	..
Scholarships	1	..	..
Bible Women	4	..	..
Dues	$190.25	..	..
Conference Expense Fund	21.40	..	..
Pledge	266.75	..	..
Thank Offering	25.20	..	..
Bible Women	240.00	..	..
Scholarships	40.00	..	..
Mite Boxes	11.30	..	..
Specials	17.75	..	..
Contingent	12.35	..	..
Total	$825.00		

MRS. U. L. MILLSAPS, District Secretary.

TREASURER'S REPORT—FOREIGN DEPARTMENT.

ALEXANDRIA DISTRICT.

Alexandria—

Dues	$16.20	
Expense Fund	20.36	
Pledge	75.00	
Retirement Fund	1.15	
Ring Scholarship	40.00	
		$152.71

Bethel—

Dues	7.55	
Expense Fund	1.20	
Pledge	2.25	
Retirement Fund	.25	
		11.25

Bunkie—

Dues	30.10	
Expense Fund	3.30	

```
Pledge .. ........................................    74.42
Retirement Fund ...............................     4.30
                                                 ———— 112.12
```

   Natchitoches—
```
Dues .. ......................................    11.55
Expense Fund ...............................     3.30
Pledge .. ...................................     5.00
Retirement Fund ..............................      .50
                                                 ————  20.35
```

   Opelousas—
```
Dues .....................................    24.70
Expense Fund ...............................     6.05
Pledge ....................................    70.00
Retirement .. ...............................      .35
Scholarship ....  ..........................    60.00
                                                 ———— 161.10
```

   Simsport—
```
Dues ....  ..................................     5.55
Expense Fund ...............................      .50
Pledge ....  ................................     2.15
                                                 ————   8.20
```

```
   Total for District ..........................  $465.73
```

BATON ROUGE DISTRICT.

   Amite—
```
Dues .. ....................................     3.05    3.05
```
   Baton Rouge—
```
Dues .. .....................................    19.45
Expense Fund ...............................     3.85
Pledge .. ...................................     5.56
Retirement Fund ..............................      .45
Scholarship ....  ...........................    40.00
                                                 ————  69.31
```

   Jackson—
```
Dues ....  ..................................    10.50
Expense Fund ...............................     1.00
Pledge ....  ................................     2.00
                                                 ————  13.50
```

   Gayden-Pine Grove—
```
Dues ....  ..................................    12.90
Expense Fund ...............................     3.00
Pledge ....  .... ...........................    35.20
Iva Gayden Memorial Fund....................    40.00
Scholarships ....  ..........................    80.00
                                                 ———— 171.10
```

   Saint Francisville—
```
Dues ....  ..................................    16.80
Expense Fund ...............................     5.20
Pledge ....  ................................    25.70
Retirement Fund ..............................      .85
Trueheart Lectureship ......................     5.00
                                                 ————  53.55
```

   Saint Francisville Juvenile—
```
Dues ....  ..................................     5.65    5.65
```

Zachary—
Dues 12.75
Expense Fund .... .60
                                                        ——— 13.35

    Total for District................................... $329.51

CROWLEY DISTRICT.

Crowley—
Dues 55.10
Expense Fund 13.50
Pledge ...,. 125.00
Retirement Fund 1.65
Scholarship 40.00
                                                        ——— 235.25

    Crowley Juvenile—
Dues 12.47
Kindergarten in China............................ 12.96
                                                        ——— 25.43

Franklin—
Dues 1.20
Expense Fund .... .30
Pledge 14.10
Retirement Fund 5.00
                                                        ——— 20.60

Gueydan—
Dues 3.80
Pledge .... .20
                                                        ——— 4.00

    Lafayette—
Dues 16.45
Expense Fund 3.00
Pledge ..: 55.60
Retirement Fund 1.10
                                                        ——— 76.15

    Lake Charles—
Dues 31.10
Expense Fund 6.40
Pledge 59.80
Retirement 1.35
Scholarship 40.00
Special for Scholarship Girl..................... 3.00
                                                        ——— 141.65

    Total for District $503.08

MONROE DISTRICT.

Gilbert Juvenile—
Dues 8.95
Expense Fund 2.10
Pledge 10.00
Retirement 3.32
                                                        ——— 24.37

    Mer Rouge Juvenile—
Dues 8.85   8.85

Monroe—

Dues	36.05	
Expense	5.25	
Pledge	60.20	
Retirement	1.40	
		102.90

Monroe Juvenile—

Dues	1.45	
		1.45

Total for District .... $137.57 ·

NEW ORLEANS DISTRICT.

Carrollton—

Dues	34.00	
Expense Fund	5.95	
Pledge	107.50	
Retirement Fund	4.45	
Scholarship	40.00	
Bible Women	60.00	
		251.90

Carrollton Young People—

Dues	11.30	
Expense	1.35	
Pledge	3.45	
Retirement	.50	
Furnishing Room in Korea School	20.00	
		36.60

Felicity—

Dues	17.50	
Expense	1.80	
Pledge	8.25	
Retirement	1.70	
Special for China, Memory of J. H. Keller	100.00	
		129.25

First Church, N. O.—

Dues	43.95	
Expense	6.40	
Pledge	150.00	
Retirement Fund	5.45	
Scholarship	40.00	
		245.80

Louisiana Avenue—

Dues	22.40	
Expense Fund	1.50	
Pledge	34.35	
		58.25

Parker Memorial—

Dues	20.85	
Expense Fund	2.70	
Pledge	7.36	
Retirement Fund	.90	
		31.81

Rayne Memorial—

Dues	50.05	
Expense Fund	9.96	
Pledge	255.68	

Retirement	20.00	
Scholarship	120.00	
Bible Woman	120.00	
		575.69
Second Church—		
Dues	14.80	
Expense	.25	
Pledge	2.82	
Retirement	.05	
		17.92
Total for District...............................		$1347.22

RUSTON DISTRICT.

Gibsland Juvenile—		
Dues	2.95	
		2.95
Homer—		
Dues	22.05	
Expense Fund	3.30	
Pledge ...:	41.90	
Retirement Fund	.30	
		67.55
Minden—		
Dues	26.10	
Expense Fund	5.50	
Pledge	111.35	
Retirement Fund	2.85	
Scholarship :....	40.00	
		185.80
Ruston—		
Dues	47.30	
Expense Fund	6.80	
Pledge	51.00	
Retirement	1.57	
		106.67
Ruston Juvenile—		
Dues	3.61	
		3.61
Total for District		$366.58

SHREVEPORT DISTRICT.

Grand Cane—		
Dues :....	15.20	
Expense Fund	.60	
Pledge	11.55	
Retirement Fund	.30	
		27.65
Greenwood—		
Dues :....	22.40	
Expense Fund	1.80	
Pledge	6.15	
		30.35
Greenwood Juvenile—		
Dues .:	3.55	
Pledge	1.25	
		4.80

Keachie—
Dues 11.35
Pledge 7.20
                                                         ——— 18.55

Noel Memorial—
Dues 25.40
Pledge 37.50
                                                         ——— 62.90

Mansfield—
Dues 16.80
Expense Fund 9.60
Pledge 15.50
Retirement 17.35
                                                         ——— 59.25

Shreveport, First Church—
Dues 98.50
Expense 22.15
Pledge 205.00
Retirement 5.15
Scholarship 40.00
Bible Woman 240.00
                                                         ——— 610.80

Total for District................................. $314.30

SPECIAL CONTRIBUTIONS.

Refunded Expense Fund, Mrs. Montgomery.......... 8.00
Refunded Expense Fund, Miss A. Parker............ 4.00
Refunded Expense Fund, N. O. District............ 12.00
Shreveport Epworth League Scholarship............ 40.00
S. S. Hunter Scarritt Scholarship................ 180.00
                                                         ——— 244.00

Grand Total $4207.99
Balance from last year................................. 179.10

                                                         $4387.09

RECEIPTS.

Dues .. ..$ 862.23
Special Pledge 1719.99
Scholarships 620.00
Bible Women 420.00
Retirement Fund 82.24
Hunter Scholarship 180.00
Special to China (Memorial J. H. Keller)............. 100.00
Kindergarten in China 12.96
Special, Furnishing Room, Korea...................... 20.00
Sewing Material for Scholarship Girl................. 3.00
Trueheart Lectureship 5.00
Expense Fund 182.57

Total $4207.99
Balance from last year............................... 179.10

Grand total $4387.09

WOMAN'S MISSIONARY SOCIETY

CREDITS.

By amounts paid—

General Treasurer	$3730.78
Miss Billingsly (Secretary Training School)	180.00
New Orleans Advocate, printing minutes	72.50
Dr. Werlein, travel to Alexandria	12.50
Miss Ada Parker, travel to Alexandria	12.00
Mrs. A. F. Watkins	25.00
Mrs. Montgomery, travel and office expense	102.50
Mrs. Carre's travel to Alexandria	15.00
Mrs. Bartels, travel to Alexandria	8.50
Mrs. Sewell's travel and office expense	14.25
Mrs. Eskridge, travel and office expense	15.03
Mrs. Holt, travel and office expense	14.55
Mrs. Worrell, office expense	9.00
Mrs. Millsaps, office expense	6.00
Mrs. Keener, office expense	9.00
Mrs. Dudley, office expense	9.00
Mrs. Carter, office expense	3.00
Mrs. Holmes, office expense	3.45
For purchasing fancy work from China	12.00
Total	$4254.06
Balance on hand	133.03
Grand total	$4387.09

MRS. J. J. HOLMES, Treasurer.

May 9, 1911.

MRS. W. W. CARRE, President,
Woman's Foreign Missionary Society,
Louisiana Conference,
Methodist Episcopal Church, South,
Monroe, Louisiana.

Dear Madam:

This is to certify that I have carefully audited the books, reports, bank accounts, etc., of your Treasurer, Mrs. J. J. Holmes, and I find them well kept and all moneys received properly accounted for.

Very respectfully,
CHARLES M. ROBERTS.

FIRST ANNUAL MEETING

SPECIALS SUPPORTED BY THE LOUISIANA CONFERENCE.

BIBLE·WOMEN.

Name.	Where.	By whom.	When.
Nannie Battle	China	Shreveport Auxiliary	1899
Dorothy Wilmot	China	Mrs. R. W. Wilmot, of New Orleans	1901
Marguerite Foster	China	Mrs. L. S. Crain, of Shreveport	1903
Carrie La Prade	China	Rayne Memorial Aux	1906
Amelia McCutchen	Korea	Mrs. J. C. Foster, of Shreveport	1907
Priscilla Bentley	Korea	Carrollton Avenue Aux	1908

SCHOLARSHIPS.

Name	Where	By whom	When
Lee Dicks	Korea	Rayne Memorial Aux	1899
Mary Keener	Mexico	First Church, New Orleans	1899
Marguerite Crain	China	Shreveport Juvenile	1899
Christine Cohen	Mexico	Carrollton Avenue	1901
Belle O'Pry	Mexico	Rayne Memorial	1905
Bettie Martin	Korea	Mrs. N. R. Grigsby, of Minden, La.	1906
Ring Scholarship	Brazil	Louisiana Conference	1907
Elisa Ascanio	Mexico	Lake Charles Auxiliary	1907
Robbie Foster	Brazil	Mrs. Paul Foster, of Opelousas, La.	1907
N. E. O'Pry	Korea	Mrs. T. B. Belle, of Algiers, La	1908
Margaret Kent	China	Baton Rouge Auxiliary	1908
Sarah Burton	Brazil	Crowley Auxiliary	1908
Quina	Brazil	Mrs. Crow Girard, of Lafayette	1908
Darling Erwin	Korea	Mrs. Erwin, of Clinton	1909
Alice Cobb	Korea	Gayden Auxiliary	1909
Hattie Renfro	China	Shreveport Ep. League	1910

REPORT OF PRESS SUPERINTENDENT.

We have been unable to do all we would like to have done in this department, owing to the increased duties which fell to us in our office of Corresponding Secretary. Bulletins sent out, 1929; items furnished to our column in N. O. Christian Advocate.

MRS. CROW GIRARD.

REPORT OF YOUNG PEOPLE'S WORK.

We regret that we are obliged to report a decrease both in the number of societies and in the total membership.

Our faithful Carrollton Avenue Y. P. disbanded to work in the fourth department of the League.

The Juvenile of First Church, Shreveport, has for several months been without a lady manager and has joined forces with the Junior League.

The Ruston Juvenile disbanded in favor of the Boy Scouts and others, organized shortly before our last annual conference, owing to peculiar local conditions, did not survive long enough to send in their first reports.

Number of Y. P. auxiliaries reporting during the year, 2; Number of Juveniles reporting during the year, 7.

Financial report as follows:

Young People's—Dues, $14.25; conference expense, $1.35; pledge, $3.45; specials, $20.00: retirement fund, 50 cents. Total, $39.55.

Juvenile—Dues, $44.53; contingent, 40 cents; conference expense, $1.70; pledge, $11.25; specials, $12.96; retirement fund, $3.32. Total, $74.16.

Grand total, $113.71.

Forty letters have been written in the interest of the work and the leaflets supplied have been distributed.

MRS. BRISCOE CARTER,
Superintendent Y. P.

REPORT OF COMMITTEE ON EXTENSION OF WORK.
HOME AND FOREIGN DEPARTMENTS.

Realizing that the duty of the *whole* Church is to save the *whole* world, and that only as a united body will we win the world to Christ, therefore we recommend most heartily:

1. That all auxiliaries unite under the constitution for united societies, and that, further, wherever new auxiliaries are organized, either junior, young people or adult, that they be organized under the new constitution for union societies.

2. That the vice-presidents of children and young people be the most capable, consecrated women possible; that they will do all they can for training the young life of the Church in mission work in its broadest sense.

3. That because of the importance of the study of social conditions that fourth vice-presidents of auxiliaries be chosen

51

because of especial fitness for and interest in this work. We advise that in union societies each auxiliary fourth vice-president have two working committees—one in charge of local work, such as was done by the aid societies; the other to have charge of the social service work, including house-to-house visitation, local charity, the study of local conditions and co-operation with movements for the betterment of existing conditions.

4. We recommend that district secretaries encourage a union district meeting in place of separate meetings of the two departments.

5. That the auxiliaries urge upon the members the need of definite intercessory prayer in the meetings and in the home life; also that we cannot do God's will unless we know it; therefore the study of the Word is absolutely necessary.

6. It is of utmost importance that we realize our stewardship to God. To get this subject more on the hearts of our women we request our pastors to present to their congregations the subject of Christian stewardship in a special sermon.

7. That an hour be given to the presentation of Christian stewardship and mission study at the annual session of the conference society. That emphasis be laid upon the reading of the "Missionary Voice." An active, church-wide canvass must be made, 100,000 subscribers being necessary to make the "Voice" self-supporting. If the young life of the Church is to be interested in missions, the "Young Christian Worker" must be more widely circulated. The "King's Messenger" is also recommended.

We would urge more careful study of the leaflets sent out to us, and that there be in every auxiliary, Junior, Young People and Adult a mission study course. The use of Matthews' Social Gospel is recommended as an introductory Bible study at each meeting for both the Home and Foreign Study course.

That we continue the "Every Member" campaign during the months of September, October and November, seeking to win every woman to missions.

11. That our missionary work be presented at a public meeting at least once during the year, when members, both active and honorary, shall be solicited. We suggest that one of these public meetings be held early in the fall campaign for members.

12. That "Training School Day" be observed throughout

the conference, when the work and needs of the Scarritt Bible and Training School shall be presented.

That each delegate realize her duty to present the report of the annual meeting at the first auxiliary meeting after the annual meeting.

14.   That circulating libraries be established in each auxiliary, the press superintendent to have charge of this work.

15.   That the women of the Church throw about the students cf the State and Church schools such social and religious influences as are possible, making them feel a part of the missionary force of the Church.

16.   That each district secretary endeavor to visit the auxiliaries in her district, organizing wherever possible. That the district meeting be conducted after the plan of missionary institutes, urging representation from each church, and especially that the four vice-presidents of auxiliaries attend.

17.   That the district secretaries be a standing committee for the extension of work; that they be aided by a committee within each auxiliary; that this committee be made up of the Auxiliary President, District Secretary, Corresponding Secretary and others appointed by the Auxiliary President.

MRS. A. P. HOLT, Chairman.

REPORT OF COMMITTEE ON YOUNG PEOPLE'S WORK.

Since the Young People's and Children's work of the Missionary Council has been magnified and made a distinctive department with vice-presidents and respective conference vice-presidents, we are called upon to bestir ourselves as never before to win for our beloved cause those who belong to us by heritage. We therefore recommend:

1.   That wherever there are as many as six young people in any church, an earnest attempt should be made to organize a Young People's Missionary Society.

2.   Where there is no organization of a Home or Foreign Missionary Society, an effort should be made to have both departments represented in one organization. Where there is an organization this combined plan should be encouraged.

3.   That every auxiliary elect as first and second vice-presi-

dents, women adapted to lead the young people and children.

4. Since there is no distinctive literature published for our young people and children we recommend that the educational work for them be carried on through the bulletin, and the Young Christian Worker. The Missionary Voice, Everyland and The Gospel of the Kingdom will be found especially helpful and interesting. All of these may be ordered from the Publishing House at Nashville, through Mrs. A. L. Marshall.

5. That October be set as a special time for organizing Mission Study Classes, and that an effort be made to induce our church schools to include a Mission Study Course in their curriculum.

6. We would urge the importance of social service and investigation of local conditions according to a definite plan.

7. In college towns, local auxiliaries are uregd to have one open meeting each year for our young people in attendance upon these colleges.

8. That public meetings be held as often as practicable.

9. That our young people be urged and encouraged to send representatives to the various missionary assemblies for young people.

10. That the attention of the auxiliary officers in charge of Young People's and Children's work be called to the inspirational value of the regular missionary lesson of the Sunday school, and that they seek the closest affiliation with this missionary work in the Sunday school.

11. We recommend that especial effort be made to organize the boys for specific missionary work.

12. That Friday before Easter be set apart as a day of prayer for volunteers to the work in mission fields.

—————

REPORT OF PUBLISHING COMMITTEE.

Believing that He who said "My people perish for lack of knowledge" would have us avail ourselves of every opportunity to become intelligent workmen and women, who need not be ashamed, we recommend:

1. That the Reading Course be more urgently brought before the auxiliaries.

WOMAN'S MISSIONARY SOCIETY

2. That our literature and books be brought to the Annual Conference, where they may be purchased by the delegates, and a committee appointed at each said conference to dispose of the same.

3. That a Press Superintendent be appointed in each local auxiliary, and so reported to the State Superintendent.

4. That since we have in our Sunday schools what are known as missionary and temperance days, a committee composed of Press Superintendent, Vice-President of Children's Work and Vice-President of Young People's work, be appointed to supply the Sunday schools with facts concerning our work and that a membership canvass be inaugurated.

5. That we urge the young people to adopt their study course and subscribe for the Young Christian Workers.

6. That it be the duty of auxiliary presidents to instruct the other local officers on their various duties, at least annually.

7. That we use all space we can secure regularly, in both our church and secular papers, to advertise our work.

8. That we urge a careful and prayerful study of the Bible, from which comes our marching orders, "Go forward."

MRS. A. C. McKINNEY.

REPORT OF PARSONAGE COMMITTEE.

The following applications for aid on parsonages have been considered by your committee and been granted as follows:

	Asked for.	Granted.
Haughton, Ruston District	$100.00	$100.00
Rayne, Lafayette District	300.00	200.00
Jena, Alexlandria District	200.00	100.00

Signed:

MRS. R. W. VAUGHAN.

FINANCE COMMITTEE.

We recommend:

1. That in each church the missionary committee in its appeal to the church include in its budget the work of the women.

2. That we as an organization use our best efforts to establish in any church the plan of weekly offerings.

3. That wherever this plan is adopted a committee with the Treasurer of the Woman's Missionary Society as chairman act as a sub-committee for the collecting of the money directed to the woman's work, and to render such other aid as is possible.

4. That prayer lists of wealthy people be made for local use, that through concerted prayer their hearts may be touched for missions.

5. To create a much-needed endowment fund for the Scarritt Bible and Training School, every auxiliary be asked to contribute at least two ($2.00) dollars toward this fund.

6. That since the contingent fund is inadequate for the conference expense and publication of the minutes, we request that, at the first meeting after the annual meeting, a collection be taken in each auxiliary for this purpose.

7. That the presidents of the auxiliaries emphasize the importance of the Retirement and Relief Funds, and urge every member to make an annual offering of at least ten cents to each fund.

8. That we authorize the Secretary of the Foreign Department to make a pledge of two thousand ($2,000.00) dollars and the Secretary of the Home Department to make a pledge of one thousand ($1000.00) dollars for the conference.

MRS. R. C. HOLT, Chairman.

COMMITTEE ON BY-LAWS.

We, your committee, recommend that the following items be added to the by-laws for conference societies and numbered as follows

21. There shall be a standing committee on by-laws of seven members, who shall be the President, the two Corresponding Secretaries, the Treasurer and three members from the conference at large, to be appointed by the Executive Committee.

To this committee shall be sent all amendments to the by-laws of the conference and auxiliary societies not later than thirty days before the annual meeting of the conference society.

22. The by-laws may be amended by a two-thirds vote at any annual session of the conference.

23. The necessary expenses of the conference officers, District Secretaries, superintendents of departments and the travel-

ing expenses of conference officers, district secretaries, superintendents and speakers to the annual meeting shall be met from the treasury. .   .

24.   Each auxiliary shall be entitled to one delegate for each department.   Auxiliaries whose membership number twenty-five or over shall be entitled to one additional delegate for each department for each additional twenty-five members or fractional part thereof.

25.   A contingent fee of 30 cents per year per member shall be paid to each department of the work, 5 cents of each to be kept at home and the remainder to be sent to the Conference Treasurer for conference expenses.

MRS. S. A. MONTGOMERY, Chairman.

STANDING RULES.

1.   Applications for all specials shall be made through the Conference Corresponding Secretaries.

2.   A quiz on the minutes of the annual meeting shall be prepared each year by one of the Corresponding Secretaries and a copy mailed to the president and corresponding secretary of each auxiliary.

3.   The following items shall have a permanent place in the Conference Minutes:

(a)   The address and price of "The Missionary Voice" and "Young Christian Worker.".

(b)   The Reading Course for adult, young people and children's societies, price and publishers.

(c)   The constitution for conference, auxiliary, young people's and children's societies.

(d)   A list of the officers and managers of the Woman's Missionary Council.

4.   The Conference Treasurers shall notify the Conference Corresponding Secretaries when the money is in hand to meet specials, specifying by whom paid.

5.   At each annual meeting, where practical, public collections shall be taken for the conference work.

6.   The Conference Treasurer shall advance to the Conference Corresponding Secretaries $10.00 per quarter for office expenses.

· 7.   Stationery with the printed names of conference officers and district secretaries shall be furnished for the correspondence of the conference officers and district secretaries.

8. The annual meeting of the Conference Society shall be held after the meeting of the Missionary Council, the exact date to be fixed by the Executive Committee.

9. District secretaries and conference treasurers shall send a duplicate of their quarterly reports to the Conference President.

10. An editor and an associate editor, both living in the same town, shall be appointed by the chair to arrange and print the Conference Minutes.

RESOLUTIONS.

In the name of the Woman's Missionary Society of the Louisiana Conference, we present the following resolutions:

First. We wish to express our sincere appreciation to Rev. R. H. Wynn and his estimable wife for their untiring efforts in behalf of this meeting.

Second. We extend our heartfelt thanks to the faithful committee of ladies and young men for their promptness in meeting the trains and assigning us comfortable homes; also to our hostesses who have so graciously opened their homes to us, we extend hearty thanks for their charming hospitality.

Third. We would especially thank the ladies for the elegant reception given in honor of the delegates at the hospitable home of Rev. and Mrs. S. S. Keener. The perfume of the flowers, the music, the sweet concourse of many friends, and the delicious refreshments will all remain a pleasant memory in the days to come.

Fourth. We remember with appreciation the eloquent words of welcome spoken by Rev. R. H. Wynn and Mrs. M. A. McHenry; we wish to express our appreciation to the organist and choir for the beautiful music which has been rendered.

Fifth. That we are greatly indebted to Miss Belle Bennett, president of the Woman's Missionary Council, for information and inspiration given us the first two days of our session, assuring her that our earnest prayers go with her for her continued strength of body and mind; both of which she used so freely, faithfully and judiciously for the betterment of mankind.

Sixth. We are indebted to Rev. N. E. Joyner, Rev. R. W. Vaughan, Rev. Albert Lutz and Miss Margaret Ragland for able addresses on subjects of interest.

Seventh. Recognizing the power of the press and the great assistance it has given us in our general work, we would thank the daily papers of Monroe for giving accounts of our meetings in their columns.

Eighth. We are deeply grateful to Rev. Paul M. Brown for his splendid sermon on Sunday morning.

Ninth. To Miss Mabel Head, educational secretary of the Woman's Missionary Council, we express our appreciation for her presence and helpful words which give us a broadening of ideas concerning the great cause of missions.

Tenth. In closing, we would reiterate our sincere gratitude to the good people of Monroe for their cordial hospitality, and many acts of kindness extended us during our stay in their city and to any others who have contributed to the success of this meeting, we extend our heartfelt appreciation.

MRS. D. C. WORRELL.

RESOLUTION.

In view of the faithful and efficient service of the retiring officers of the Home Mission and Foreign Mssionary Societies, we move a rising vote of thanks be tendered them. Carried.

MRS. CROW GIRARD,
MRS. R. C. HOLT.

REPORT OF THE FIRST ANNUAL SESSION, WOMAN'S MISSIONARY COUNCIL.

On May 19 to 29, at St. John's Methodist Church, St. Louis, there were gathered together the workers in Home and Foreign Mission Societies in the first annual session of the Woman's Missionary Council. It will have an historical setting as one of the beginnings of the answer to Christ's prayer, "that we may all be one." The dominant note of this, as it was of the Edinburgh meeting, being "a united body to conquer in Christ's name." The results will reach to the end of time. Born of prayer, fostered thus, and carried out, day by day, as one great expression of hearts' desires to do the Master's will, not alone in these days when sharp lines were to be drawn, but in the work of the future—is it to be wondered that the presence of God was so manifest to those interested in Samaria, in Judea, in Jerusalem, and to those who will go to the uttermost parts of the earth?

"The Council Daily," one of Miss Gibson's happy thoughts, and the splendid work of the St. Louis women, has gone out to many of our interested women. The issue was so successful that it was made a permanent feature of the Council meetings.

At the opening service Wednesday evening Dr. James Lee. pastor of St. John's; Dr. Wainwright, Presiding Elder of the St. Louis District (who will return to Korea in the summer), and Dr. W. W. Pinson, General Secretary of the Board of Missions, administered the Holy Sacrament to those gathered from the earth's corners. The address of the evening, by Dr. Pinson, brought the importance of unified action strongly before his hearers. The business of this, the twentieth century, is to make a "brotherhood of the world that the nineteenth century has made only a neighborhood." That success in breaking the solid phalanx of heathenism will be accomplished only by an equally solid line of Christians who are laboring at home as one great body, using every effort to set the light of Christ where darkness dwells.

Miss Belle Bennett, President of the Women's Missionary Council, delivered her first annual message to the Council after the necessary preliminary business of Thursday morning. She spoke of the larger life to which we are called, since our work has been united with that of the Parent Board, and of the honor the womanhood of our church has had put upon it, in being admitted to its administrative council. Despite the unrest of the. year, collections have increased. Housing and equipping our institutions, at home and abroad, with the very best, should be our policy, to be more intensive in work and workers. Vocational training was emphasized. Study must be made of SOCIAL conditions if we are to keep pace with the times, and if we would make the future harvest days cleaner, richer and more glorious.

Reports of the secretaries and division managers brought in much of interest—much to be worked for. Mrs. J. B. Cobb, Secretary of the Foreign Department, reported an increase of 518 auxiliaries and 1204 members, making a total in juvenile, young people and adult societies of 99,626. Some gifts are recorded, but it is desired that prayer lists be made of the wealthy people of every place, these prayer lists to be used locally. Miss Bennett also asked for these lists, that through this concerted prayer those to whom wealth has been entrusted may be made to realize their stewardship and that large gifts to missions may be resultant.

Schools everywhere are in good condition. While relief has come to the overcrowded condition of the Susan Bond Wilson school in Sungkiang, by the new dormitory, it calls for more teachers. In Shanghai, McTyeire *must* have more room. Every kind of mission work is carried on in Soochow. The Industrial School there furnishes support for ninety women, forty-two of whom were touched for Christ this year. Steps will be taken toward an interdenominational college in Kiangsu Province for higher education of girls. Possibly one of the loudest calls is for kindergarten teachers and equipment. The government is seeking them—even to furnishing money for the training of four in Miss Atkinson's School at Soochow. While at least six missionaries were called for, only three could be sent. A new era in China is indicated by the word from Mrs. Hearn that over one hundred delegates and visitors from Shanghai to Changchow, to the Bible Women's Institute, went and returned for a *single* fare in a *special car*—a gospel car in this celestial empire.

Soul-winning in Korea is gratifying in numbers. The new Lucy Cunningham School at Wonsan will not be ready before fall. Three day schools will be opened at Seoul, as they supply needs that boarding schools cannot. The Bible Women's School is also to be a reality. To win the million souls this year fifty missionaries are necessary. The Council sent only six of that number. So, while we are praying for the million souls, shall we not also plead for the needed workers to win them?

Brazil's great need is better equipment. We are asked to send a jubilee offering of $50,000 to build a girls' school at Rio de Janeiro. The "week of prayer" offering and young people's gifts will go to augment this. A gift of $10,000 will come for the Rio school if we raise the remainder. Rio is the strategic point in Brazil and must be cared for by a splendid school. The Martha Watts annex will be built this year. A kindergarten teacher and her equipment is supplied, for the first time, and the work thereby enlarged will bring in scores who have been kept away. Misses Jarett, Epps, Barton, Ferguson, Simpson and Schalch, a native Brazilian, were assigned to Brazil.

Although Mexico is in such a state of turmoil politically, school work has not been affected. Our prayers should ascend daily for these, our missionaries and representatives, who so need strength and protection even at this very hour. Three new workers go to the help of the few. Mrs. A. C. McLendon, long a worker there, retires, receiving an interest in the retirement fund. Investigations will be made concerning the possibility of a larger work in Mexico City, the need being imperative.

The Indian work is so poorly housed and a change of location so needful that a commission was appointed, consisting of members from both departments, to look into the needs and advisability of transferring the Indian work to the Home Department.

To create a much needed endowment fund for the Scarritt Bible and Training School, every auxiliary is asked to send *at least* $2.00 for this fund.

The total amount appropriated for the Foreign Department was $269,288.00. The total collections in Foreign Departments were $278,973.07, an increase of $18,000.

The Secretary of the Home Department, Mrs. R. W. McDonall, reports a gain of 237 auxiliaries, 5741 members, or a total of 101,663, with the total collections $206,512.45, an increase of $11,000, this not including amount for local work.

One hundred and eighty parsonages have been aided. The Board of Church Extension will take care of this branch of work hereafter, granting one-fifth of its entire funds to parsonages. One thousand three hundred and twenty-five boxes, valued at $39,172.06, were sent. Eleven connectional schools with 77 teachers, 1574 students, at a cost of $49,286.30, are maintained—this for instructing the Cubans, the mountain girls and boys, for industrial training among the unfortunate and unprotected of our girls and for the negroes, and for the foreigners on our shores.

The Sue Bennett Memorial School, London, Ky., has been made agent for university extension work along agricultural lines. The new dormitory is almost completed. The grade of work done here is most excellent.

The new Mary Bruce Hall, Ruth Hargrove Institute, Key

West, is nearing completion. Brevard Institute, Brevard, N. C., has so outgrown its present home that larger accommodations are imperative. The "Week of Prayer" offering from the Home Department will go to meet this need. The foundation for the new Ann Browder Home and School, at Dallas, Texas, is being laid.

December 23rd being Miss Mary Helm's birthday, it is hoped that auxiliaries will observe the day appropriately, making an offering for the Mary Helm Chapel, Alameda, Cal.

Women of the church are urged to throw about the State and Church schools such social and religious influences as are possible, even to having Home Mission dormitories for those of our boys and girls leaving home for higher education. Competition at home, as abroad, is with splendidly equipped government schools, so our Christian schools must offer similar advantages if they command the patronage and answer the purpose for which they were established.

The total amount appropriated for the Home Department was $79,069.

We must also keep in close touch with the college young people around us, making them feel a part of the missionary force of the Church. Specific objects for their contributions will be published during the year.

Expressive of the spirit of unity and purpose is the pledge from the South Georgia Conference, Home and Foreign Departments, to support Miss Mary De Bardeleben, our first missionary to the negroes.

While increases are noted both in membership and finances and we are grateful for them, it is urged that each auxiliary will put forth every effort to make successful the "Every member campaign" in October and November, to win every woman in the Church to missions.

The joint report of the Committee on Estimates and Extension, Home and Foreign Departments, recommend:

1. That an hour be given to the presentation of Christian Stewardship and Mission Study at the annual session of each conference society.

2. That in each church the Missionary Committee in its appeal to the Church include in its budget the work of the women.

3. That we, as an organization, use our best efforts to

establish in every church the plan of weekly offerings.

4. That wherever this plan is adopted a committee from the Woman's Missionary Society offer themselves as a sub-committee for the collection of the money directed to their work, and to render such other aid as is possible.

5. That we request our pastors to present to their congregations the subject of Christian Stewardship in a special sermon, and that the editors of the Church papers be asked to present the subject through the columns of their papers. The time for this special effort to be decided later, according to the plans of the program committee.

The First Vice-President, Mrs. J. E. Leith, in charge of the children's work, made clear the importance of children at work in saying that "until there is an organization for the training of children in every church in the whole of Southern Methodism we have not done our full duty." The auxiliary first vice-president in each local church should seek the closest affiliation with the Sunday school and its missionary committee. This department will soon have a suitable pin for the children.

The same strong plea for the enlistment of the young life of the Church came from Mrs. J. E. Grubbs, Second Vice-President in charge of young people's work. Their motto, "Prayer and pains through faith in Jesus Christ will do anything," we hope will be effectual, even to getting the need of the hour—"leaders." Wherever as many as six young people are found in any church a serious effort should be made to organize them. They are to have a year book and special leaflets. October is set aside as a special time for organizing mission study classes. Our young people are urged to send representatives to the various missionary assemblies for young people. Leaders are urged to organize boys and young men in mission bands, appealing to the "gang" spirit for unity. The Sunday school can be used successfully for enlisting the young. Friday before Easter shall be a special prayer day for volunteers for both the Home and Foreign work.

Too much emphasis cannot be laid upon the "Department of Christian Stewardship and Mission Study," represented by Mrs, J. W. Perry, the Third Vice-President in charge. The "Every Member Campaign"—seeking to enlist each church member in the support of the gospel by a regular weekly offering—

is one of this department's desires. That our purpose in life might be enlarged to taking thought first for the service of Christ in material things, and to serving our fellows, the name of this department has been changed from "Tithing" to that of "Stewardship." The millennial dawn will be near when, in every church, men and women will be studying together the great world questions of humanity's needs, and then "seeking through guidance of the Holy Spirit to use whatever of time, means, opportunity or graces the Father has entrusted to their care, for the relief and elevation of mankind." What joy it will be when man realizes "that the more he denies himself the more he shall obtain from God."

The Editorial Secretary, Mrs. A. L. Marshall, brought in a report whose key note was "Prayer." Of the sixty-four pages contained in the Missionary Voice, the newly merged union of the "Missionary Advocate," "Our Homes" and "Go Forward," thirty-two pages are devoted to the two departments of our work. The united subscription list was nearly 50,000, but this, at the present low price of 50 cents, is not enough to pay expenses. If the women would keep to their ideal of barring advertisements and yet retain this price, we must make or help make an active church-wide canvass, to double the present subscription list. More use of church and secular papers is urged for spreading missionary information. Leaflets should be revised and printed in better form. Mrs. Cobb and Mrs. McDonall will send out some bulletins. There will be no more club rates given for the Young Christian Worker—the uniform price being 25 cents.

Literature giving best methods of advertising meetings and planning for the work of a publicity committee will be published, so that the best possible results may be obtained from "Field Workers." Each auxiliary president will get one year book of the same plan of correlated work of this year and one hand book, the combination of the Foreign Mission "Hand Book" and the Home Mission "Help for Home Mission Workers."

Mrs. Butler and Miss Helm are asked to prepare the first of a series of booklets for children—this to give an account of the missionary work in both departments.

Miss Head, the Educational Secretary, reports much accomplished. The whole Church last year reported 925 missionary study classes, numbering 12,487. This year there are 1108 classes, numbering 15,313. In the woman's work alone there are 11,484, which is only 1003 less than the *whole Church* reported last year. The mottoes, "The Evangelization of the World in This Generation," "We Can Do It If We Will," "We Can Do It and We Will," all are possible if we add to these "If We Know the Facts of Missions."

The inspirational message from the Field Secretary, Miss Davies, set two watchwords for the year: "Definite," "Adequate," and a jubilee meeting with a jubilee offering from every auxilary. Our women are released from the bondage which held our grandmothers, that we might spend these freed six hours in service to Christ and men.

The Department of Social Service and Local Work has in it possibilities of infinite influences for good. Even the smallest auxiliary in the country town should take up the work. It was said that "Social service" means "heal the wounds of the afflicted, as the Samaritan did, but do not stop there, follow after the robbers and clear them out. Make the way from Jericho to Jerusalem safe."

Choose fourth vice-presidents with fitness for and interest in the work. It is suggested that we have two working committees—one to have charge of the local work purely, and the other in charge of the social service work, including house to house visitation, local charity, study of local conditions and co-operation with movements for the betterment of existing conditions.

In the memorial service was read John's wonderful picture of the Holy City, into which some of the beloved workers of the ranks have entered this year—Mrs. J. W. Humbert, Miss Marcia Marvin, Miss Virginia Cloud, Mrs. Mary N. Carr, Miss Jennie Snider. Of them all it might be said that their joys lay in service, their thoughts for others; their strength, the Master; their peace, the Christ.

The annual sermon preached by Bishop Hendrix on John 1:18 treated of the spiritual law of gravitation, drawing Christ unto the bosom of God. Bishop Mouzon's sermon at Centenary, from Romans 1:14, showed every man's debt unpaid—unless, as Paul, his life be given in service to Christ and to man.

"Light" was the idea upon which was built the beautiful afternoon rally program for the children.

The evening services, given largely to addresses from deaconesses and the number of returned missionaries, were full of interest.

Nothing more beautiful and impressive will ever be witnessed than the consecration services, when those forty-eight young women were set apart for the Master's service, twenty as deaconesses, nine as city missionaries and nineteen for foreign fields. Miss Bennett's charge to these latter came home to every one in that vast audience. "If Christ is not as real to you as I am, if you do not believe in a supernatural Savior, do not go. Your message will be of no avail, your life cannot endure to the end." As a number of the girls told of the influences which had led them to this hour there was not a dry eye—not a heart that was asking "Have I done what I could? If not, I will go with them in God's way, and that the shortest, to the slums, the mountains, to Mexico, to Korea—by the throne of God." Miss Gibson's prayer of consecration, as she laid her hands upon the bowed heads of those to go to the "uttermost parts," was most beautiful.

The "Hour of Intercession" came in the midst of the day's business to call us from the works of Martha to be with the Marys—in the heavenly places with Christ Jesus. So sharply drawn were the lines at times that we needed the moments when, with closed doors and a hush upon our hearts, we waited upon God to intercede for others." . This intercession, which is the highest service known to man, is unlike them all—it is superior, knowing no limitations. The needs of every land and every people, our joys, their sorrows—for they have few joys—the miner, the Chinese woman, the unfortunate girls from our very homes, the negro, the Mohammedan—all are real to us now, that we have laid them and will continue to plead for them at the Father's throne.

The all important question of unification which was discussed from the first day to the last, if not at all times, certainly whenever it could creep in, I have left to the end because it was the last to be settled and really, for some, is not settled yet. Our decision brings, however, "The peace that is of the nature of a conquest, for then both parties are subdued and neither party loser." Union of the two departments of missionary work, "Home" and "Foreign," cannot be forced upon any auxiliary or conference, but it is most heartily recommended. The basis of membership dues in the united societies will be 10 cents to either the Home or Foreign Department, or 20 cents for both. Opportunities to be given for the free will offerings and for pledges and each auxiliary to raise the amount necessary for its local work.

The officers in the conference and auxiliaries will be a President, four Vice-Presidents, two Corresponding Secretaries, one or more Recording Secretaries and one or more Treasurers. The four Vice-Presidents will have charge respectively of the "Children," "Young People," "Stewardship and Mission Study," "Social Service and Local Work." Membership in the junior division of the Young People's Department is based upon the new and higher ideal—giving regularly, prayer, service and a stated offering, the funds to be divided equally between the two departments. Mite box offerings from the juniors will be divided 60 per cent. to foreign work, 40 per cent. to the home.

There will of necessity be two constitutions. The one formerly used by all separate Home and Foreign Missionary Societies, and this new united constitution, which we hope every Louisiana auxiliary will adopt at once. Whenever organizations are effected in the future—all Juvenile and Brigades, all Young People's Societies, all new Adults—the united plan is urged. We must face the world a united body, one in Jesus, for Christ and for the world. Let the council motto be ours: "Ye are my witnesses in Jerusalem, in Judea and in all Samaria. and to the uttermost parts of the earth."

With the reading of Psalm 97 by the President, the singing of the council hymn, "Lead On, O King Eternal!" and prayer by Dr. Wainwright, the first council session was ended.

It is said that "not alone to know but to act according to thy knowledge, is thy destination. Not for indolent contemplation and study of thyself, nor for brooding over emotions of piety; no, for action was existence given thee; thy actions, and thy actions alone, determine thy *worth*." With this in mind

"We follow, not with fears, O King Eternal,
For gladness breaks like morning
    Where'er thy face appears;
Thy cross is lifted o'er us,
    We journey in its light;
The crown awaits the conquest;
    Lead on. O Lord of Might!"

CONSTITUTION OF CONFERENCE SOCIETIES.

1. In each annual conference there shall be organized a Conference Society, auxiliary to the Woman's Missionary Council.

2. The object of this society is to plan and direct the woman's missionary work of the conference.

3. The Conference Society shall consist of one or more delegates from each auxiliary, one or more district secretaries from each district, a superintendent of press work and the following officers: A president, four vice-presidents, two corresponding secretaries, a recording secretary, one or more treasurers. These officers shall be elected by ballot at the annual meeting.

BY-LAWS FOR CONFERENCES.

1. The conference officers elected by ballot shall constitute an Executive Committee to transact business in the intervals of the annual sessions. Three shall constitute a quorum.

2. Conference officers shall be nominated by a committee named by the Executive Committee, composed of one or more representatives from each district. This does not debar the parliamentary privilege of nominations from the floor after the committee's report has been presented.

3. The district secretaries and conference superintendents shall be nominated by a committee composed of the President and Corresponding Secretaries and Treasurers, and shall be elected by acclamation.

4. An alternate from each department shall be elected at each annual session to attend the session of the Woman's Missionary Council.

5. Each conference society shall adopt a plan for raising a fund to meet the expenses of the conference.

6. The Conference Society shall make its appropriations in annual session from the half of the regular membership fund of the Home Department, subject to its direction. These appropriations to be contingent upon the concurrence of the Woman's Missionary Council.

7. The President shall preside at all meetings of the Conference Society and of the Executive Committee and actively advance the interest of the society.

8. The Vice-Presidents shall, in their order, perform the duties of the President in her absence.

9. The First Vice-President shall have charge of the children's work, and shall make a quarterly report to the First Vice-President of the Woman's Missionary Council, and to the Conference Corresponding Secretary.

The Second Vice-President shall have charge of the young people's work, and shall report quarterly to the Second Vice-President of the Woman's Missionary Council and Corresponding Secretary of the Conference Society.

The Third Vice-President shall promote Christian stewardship and mission study, and shall report quarterly to the Third Vice-President of the Woman's Missionary Council and Corresponding Secretary of the Conference Society.

The Fourth Vice-President shall develop the work of social service and shall report quarterly to the Fourth Vice-President of the Woman's Missionary Council and Corresponding Secretary of Conference Society.

10. The Corresponding Secretaries shall conduct the correspondence of the society and supply the auxiliaries with information and with literature. They shall use all practicable means for the organization of adult, young people's and children's auxiliaries in every charge of the conference and forward a detailed report of each organization to the Corresponding Secretaries of the Woman's Missionary Council, to whom they shall also send quarterly reports by the 15th day of the first month of each quarter. They shall make to the Conference Society a report of the preceding session of the Woman's Missionary Council and such other reports as that body may desire. They shall sign all drafts on the treasury.

11. The Recording Secretary shall give notice of all meetings of the Conference Society and of the Executive Committee, and keep the minutes of the same on record.

12. The Treasurer shall receive all funds of the society, keeping a book account with each auxiliary and submitting the same annually to an auditor. She shall send itemized reports promptly on the 15th day of the first month of each quarter to the Treasurer of the Woman's Missionary Council, therewith transmitting such funds as are collected for the general treasury. She shall also send an itemized statement to the Conference Corresponding Secretary.

13. The District Secretary shall organize auxiliaries, and use every available means to promote the advancement of the Woman's Missionary Societies in their districts. They shall present a report of the work at the District Conference, and shall hold annual meetings in the district (composed of delegates from the auxiliaries), and all day meetings whenever practicable. If the conference so directs the District Secretaries shall conduct the correspondence with auxiliaries, and send a quarterly report to the Conference Corresponding Secretaries, and a copy of the same to the President of the Conference Society. It shall be their duty to do all in their power to obtain subscribers to the Missionary Voice and Young Christian Worker.

14. The Conference Society may elect superintendents to co-operate with the superintendents of the council. They shall send quarterly reports of their work to the General Superintendent of their department by the 15th day of the first month of each quarter.

15. Conference and auxiliary societies shall not project new work in the mission fields, nor respond to special calls for aid, without approval of the Woman's Missionary Council.

16. The regular dues of the auxiliary societies—adult, young people and children—also pledge funds and funds contributed to make life members, honorary members and life patrons, shall not be devoted to specific work.

17. The thank offering during the Week of Prayer shall be applied to some specific object to be determined each year by the Woman's Missionary Council in annual session.

18. The first meeting of the fiscal year of the auxiliaries shall be made a pledge meeting, at which time voluntary pledges shall be made by the members and a report of the same be forwarded to the Conference Corresponding Secretaries.

19. The Conference Society may make such by-laws as the work demands, provided they do not conflict with those made by the council.

20. During the annual meetings a half hour at noon shall be set aside for devotional services.

21. (a) There shall be a standing committee on by-laws of seven members, who shall be the President, the two Corresponding Secretaries, the Treasurer and three members from the conference at large, to be appointed by the Executive Committee.

(*b*)   To this committee shall be sent all amendments to by-laws of the Conference Society and auxiliaries not later than thirty days before the council meeting of the Conference Society.

22.   The by-laws may be amended by a two-thirds vote at any annual session.

23.   The necessary expense of the conference officers, district secretaries, superintendents of departments and the traveling expenses of conference officers, district secretaries, superintendents and speakers to the annual session of the Conference Society shall be met from the treasury.

24.   Each auxiliary shall be entitled to one delegate for each department.   Auxiliaries whose membership numbers twenty-five or over shall be entitled to one additional delegate for each department for each additional twenty-five members or fractional part thereof.

25.   A contingent fee of 30 cents per year per member shall be paid to each department of the work, 5 cents of each to be kept at home and the remainder to be sent to the Conference Treasurer for conference expenses.

AUXILIARY SOCIETIES.

Any number of women may become an auxiliary to the Woman's Missionary Conference Society by adopting the following constitution and by-laws and electing the officers therein provided.

CONSTITUTION FOR AUXILIARIES.

1.   This society shall be called the Woman's Missionary Society of the.....................................auxiliary to ....Conference Society of the Woman's Missionary Council of the Methodist Episcopal Church, South.

2.   The object of this society shall be to hasten the coming of the kingdom of God in the United States and non-Christian lands by enlisting the women, young people and children in a study of the needs of the world and in active missionary service, by raising funds for the evangelization of mission fields at home and abroad, for the maintenance of the institutions under the care of the Women's Missionary Council for the betterment of civic and social conditions, and for meeting neighborhood needs.

3. Any one may become a member of this society by giving regularly prayer, service and monthly dues of 10 cents to either department or 20 cents to both. Opportunities shall be given for pledges and free-will offerings, to be directed by the donors to such objects as have been authorized by the Woman's Missionary Council.

4. Any one may become a life member of either department of the society by the payment to the general fund of $25.00 for this specific purpose.

5. The officers of the society shall be a President, four Vice-Presidents, two Corresponding Secretaries, one or more Recording Secretaries, one or more Treasurers, who shall constitute an Executive Committee of the society.

Each auxiliary may raise the amount necessary for its local work.

6. The society shall hold at least one monthly meeting for educational and inspirational purposes, and one for the transaction of business. Other meetings may be held for Bible study and the varying phases of mission work. At the last meeting of the fiscal year there shall be the annual election of officers. At the following meeting there shall be full reports of the year's work, installation of officers and consideration of plans for work for the new year.

BY-LAWS FOR AUXILIARIES.

1. The President shall preside at all meetings of the society and shall actively advance its interests. At her request or in her absence the Vice-President shall assume her duties.

2. The First Vice-President shall have charge of the children's work.

The Second Vice-President shall have charge of the young people's work.

The Third Vice-President shall promote Christian stewardship and mission study.

The Fourth Vice-President shall develop the work of social service and local work.

These officers shall co-operate with the conference officers having the same work in charge, and shall report to them quarterly.

3. The Corresponding Secretaries shall conduct the correspondence of the society and send to the District Secretaries full reports by the first day of each quarter. They shall also send annually to the District Secretaries and Conference Corresponding Secretaries the names and addresses of the officers of the auxiliary. They shall send their books to the district meeting for examination.

4. The Recording Secretary shall keep a record of the regular and called meetings and see that each meeting is propeily announced.

5. The Treasurer shall collect all moneys of the society, keep an account of the same and remit to the Conference Treasurer by the first day of each quarter, giving an itemized statement of the amounts, a duplicate of the same to be furnished the Auxiliary Corresponding Secretary. The books of the Treasurer shall be audited annually.

6. The society shall elect an agent for the Missionary Voice and a Superintendent of Press Work.

7. Superintendents of Bureaus shall be elected as needed.

8. The Vice-Presidents, Secretaries, Treasurers, Agents and Superintendents shall make written reports at the monthly business meeting.

YOUNG PEOPLE'S SOCIETIES.

CONSTITUTION.

1. This society shall be called the Young People's Society of...................., auxiliary to...................... Conference Society of the Woman's Missionary Council, Methodist Episcopal Church, South.

2. The object of this society shall be to hasten the coming of the kingdom of God in the United States and non-Christian lands by enlisting the young people in active missionary service, by raising funds for the evangelization of mission fields at home and abroad, for the maintenance of the institutions under the care of the Woman's Missionary Council, for the betterment of civic and social conditions and for the relief of neighborhood needs.

3. Any one between the ages of fourteen and twenty-two may become a member of ths society by giving regularly prayer,

service, and a stated offering to missions. Opportunities will be given for pledges for special work, and free-will offerings to be used as directed by donors to such objects as are authorized by the Woman's Missionary Council.

'The membership fund shall be divided as follows: Fifty per cent to the Foreign Department, fifty per cent to the Home Department. No other funds are subject to this division.

4. Any one may become a life member of the society by the payment to the general fund of ten dollars for this specific purpose.

5. The officers of the society shall be a President, four Vice-Presidents, one or more Corresponding Secretaries, a Recording Secretary, one or more Treasurers, who shall constitute an Executive Committee of the society

6. The society shall hold at least one monthly meeting for educational and inspirational purposes, and for the transaction of business. Other meetings may be held for Bible study and the varying phases of mission work. At the last meeting of the fiscal year there shall be the annual election of officers. At the following meeting there shall be full reports of the year's work, installation of officers and consideration of plans for work for the new year.

BY-LAWS.

1. The President shall preside at the meetings of the society, and in every way advance its interests. In her absence one of the Vice-Presidents shall preside.

2. The First Vice-President shall assist the First Vice-President of the adult auxiliary in superintending the Children's Department.

The Second Vice-President shall be agent of the missionary periodicals of the Council and Press Superintendent.

The Third Vice-President shall promote Christian stewardship and mission study.

The Fourth Vice-President shall develop the work of social service and local work.

3. The Corresponding Secretaries shall conduct the correspondence of the society and make quarterly reports to the Vice-President of the conference and to the District Secretary, to whom they shall send annually the names and addresses of their officers.

4. The Recording Secretary shall keep a record of the regular and called meetings, and see that each meeting is properly announced.

5. The Treasurer shall collect all funds of the society, keeping a book account of the same, and remit to the Conference Treasurer by the first day of each quarter. She shall send a duplicate report to the Second Vice-President of the conference, and also furnish the Corresponding Secretaries of her auxiliary with a statement of the amounts remitted. The books of the Treasurer shall be audited.

THE CHILDREN'S DEPARTMENT.

In this department the children shall be organized for the foreign and home mission work.

The object shall be to give them missionary education, train them for Christian service and cultivate in them habits of liberal and systematic giving, Bible reading and prayer.

This department shall consist of Baby and Junior Divisions, under a superintendent, who shall also be a Vice-President of the Woman's Missionary Auxiliary, whose work shall be correlated with the Conference Vice-President in charge of children's work.

BABY DIVISION.

1. Any child five years of age and under may become a member of the Baby Division of the Woman's Missionary Society upon the payment of an enrollment fee of 25 cents. Each child of the Baby Division shall be given a certificate, furnished with a mite box for voluntary offerings to be opened quarterly. Any child may become a life member of the Woman's Missionary Society by the payment of five dollars.

2. Names may be placed on the Memorial Roll by an offering to missions and by the use of the mite box in memory of the child.

3. At least once a year special meetings shall be held for the members of the Baby Division, at which time mite boxes shall be opened and a helpful program carried out.

4. The First Vice-President of adult auxiliaries shall have charge of the Baby Division.

JUNIOR DIVISION.

1. Any child between the ages of five and fourteen years

may become a member of the Junior Division of the Woman's Missionary Society by giving regularly prayer, service, and a stated offering to missions. Each child of the Junior Division shall be furnished a mite box for voluntary offerings, to be opened quarterly. Any child may become a life member of the Woman's Missionary Society by the payment of ten dollars to the general fund for this specific purpose.

2. The officers of the Junior Division shall be a President, four Vice-Presidents, Corresponding Secretary, Recording Secretary and Treasurer.

3. The Junior Division shall meet at least once a month to follow some line of study for which a program shall be furnished.

BY-LAWS.

1. The President shall preside at the meetings of the society and in every way advance its interests. In her absence one of the Vice-Presidents shall preside.

2. The First Vice-President shall help in the work of the Baby Division.

The Second Vice-President shall be the agent for the "Young Christian Worker."

The Third Vice-President shall promote Christian stewardship and mission study.

The Fourth Vice-President shall have charge of the social service and local work of the children.

3. The Corresponding Secretaries shall conduct the correspondence of the society and make quarterly reports to the Vice-President of the conference and to the District Secretaries, to whom they shall send annually the names and addresses of their officers.

4. The Recording Secretary shall keep a record of the regular and called meetings, and see that each meeting is properly announced.

5. The Treasurer shall collect all funds of the society, keep a book account of the same and remit to the Conference Treasurer quarterly. She shall send a duplicate report to the Second Vice-President of the conference and also furnish the Corresponding Secretaries of her auxiliary with a statement of the amounts remitted. The books of the Treasurer shall be audited.

BY-LAWS GOVERNING CITY MISSION WORK.

In all our cities and towns where two or more Auxiliaries of the Woman's Home Mission Society exist, whether in one or several Churches, they may unite for the promotion of city missions, under the title of a "Board of City Missions." But there shall not be in any city more than one such Board.

1. There shall be a Board of City Missions, consisting of three or more members from each co-operating Auxiliary Society, to be chosen by said Auxiliaries at the first regular meeting in January of each year. The Conference officers residing in the city, the preachers in charge of the Churches in which the Auxiliaries are located, and the presiding elder of the district may be advisory members.

2. The Board shall elect at its first meeting in February of each year a President, two Vice-Presidents, a Secretary and a Treasurer.

3. The Board shall hold at least one regular meeting each month. It shall be authorized with the approval of the executive officers of the Woman's Missionary Council to choose and employ missionaries and fix their salaries.

4. It shall employ as missionaries only those whose testimonials have been considered and approved by the executive officers of the Woman's Missionary Council.

5. All appointments of missionaries made at the Annual Meeting of the Woman's Missionary Council, or by the Standing Committee on City Missions during the year, shall continue until the next Annual Meeting of the Woman's Council, and shall be binding upon both the missionaries and the City Boards employing them. This contract cannot be broken, except for reasons as shall be regarded as good and sufficient by the Committee on City Missions.

6. A monthly report shall be made to each Auxiliary by its representatives.

7. An annual report of the work shall be made to the District Conference.

8. The Board shall apportion to each Auxiliary the amount necessary to be paid by it for salaries of those employed and other current expenses.

9. The Board shall urge the Auxiliaries to secure funds by

private subscriptions and other suitable methods for support of the work, to collect promptly and pay to the Treasurer of the Board.

10. The Board shall also report annually its work to its Conference Society and to the Woman's Board through the General Secretary.

11. City missions under the auspices of the Woman's Missionary Council shall be divided into two classes, according to their ability to support and conduct mission work.

Class A shall consist of Settlement Homes where the City Mission Board can pay regularly not less than $100 a month for current expenses. To these the Woman's Board shall appropriate 10 per cent. on money expended for current expenses the previous year and reported by voucher to the General Treasurer. Through the Standing Committee on City Missions it shall have control in the appointment of one or more workers, the character and amount of work done, and the location of the house. The Head Residents of these Homes shall be women of experience and training, and have full charge of the internal affairs of the Home and superintend the work of the other residents. The work of the Homes shall, if possible, be so correlated with that of the nearest Methodist Church as to make this Church the center of its operations and the conservator of its results.

Class B shall consist of those missions where the City Board is able to pay regularly not less than $60, or as much as $100 a month for current expenses. As this amount is not sufficient to maintain a Settlement Home, this class of missionary work shall not be so designated, and the forms of work undertaken shall be limited to such as the funds make possible of success. The missionary shall not be required to keep house or to live in the community wherein she works, but near enough to give attention to its demands. The work shall be carried on wherever possible or desirable in the nearest Methodist Church; or, if that is not possible, in close correlation with it. To this class of work the Woman's Bard shall appropriate 10 per cent on money expended during the previous year which has been reported by voucher to the General Treasurer, and shall appoint the missionary.

FOREIGN MISSION STUDY COURSES FOR 1911.

FOR ADULTS.

"Western Women in Eastern Lands," by Helen Barrett Montgomery. Price, in paper, 30 cents (postage, 7 cents); in cloth, 50 cents (postage, 7 cents).

FOR YOUNG PEOPLE.

"Korea in Transition," by J. S. Gale. Price, in paper, 35 cents (postage, 5 cents); cloth, 50 cents (postage, 7 cents).

FOR CHILDREN.

"The Finding Out Club," by Helen Barrett Montgomery. Postpaid, 25 cents.

HOME MISSION READING COURSE.

FOR AUXILIARIES.

"The Price of Power," by Stuart Holding. Price, 50 cents (postage, 7 cents).

"From Darkness to Light" (for adults), by Mary Helm. Cloth, 50 cents (postage, 7 cents); paper, 30 cents (postage, 7 cents).

"The Upward Path" (for young people), by Mary Helm. Cloth, 50 cents (postage, 7 cents). paper, 35 cents.

"The Pioneer" (for Brigades). Crowell. Paper, 25 cents.

"The Immigrant Tide." Steiner. Cloth, $1.50 net.

FOR CITY MISSION BOARDS.

"The Survey." Price, $2. (A weekly published at 105 East Twenty-Second Street, New York.)

"The Bitter Cry of the Children." Spargo. Cloth, $1.25.

FOR WORKERS APPOINTED BY THE BOARD.

"Record of Christian Work." (A monthly published at East Northfield, Mass.) Price, $1.

"The Survey." (Weekly.) Price, $2.

"The Bitter Cry of the Children." Spargo. Price, $1.25.

"Memoirs of Brainerd." Sherwood. Price, 75 cents.

MISSION STUDY COURSE, 1911-12.

FOR ADULT AUXILIARIES (Foreign).

"The Light of the World," by Robert E. Speer.

FOR ADULT AUXILIARIES (Home).

"The Conservation of National Ideals," by different authors. (H. M. Council.)

FOR YOUNG PEOPLE.

"Advance in the Antilles" (Grose), and "A country Church."

FOR CHILDREN.

"Best Things in America."

In addition to these, use Mathews' "Social Gospel" as an introductory Bible study, and "Social Evils in Non-Christian Lands" (Dennis) in connection with the books in the Foreign Study Course.

Order from Methodist Publishing House, 810 Broadway, Nashville, Tenn.